HISTORY OF
AVIATION
MILITARY AIR POWER

Often overshadowed in the history books by its predecessor, the F-86 Sabre of Korean War Fame, the North American F-100 Super Sabre is entitled to its own place in aviation history as the first level-supersonic aeroplane to be built in quantity. It has remained in continuous service with various air forces since 1954 —yet not so many years earlier the sound 'barrier' confronted designers and pilots with technical problems and physical risk

HISTORY OF
AVIATION
MILITARY AIR POWER

Edited by John W R Taylor and Kenneth Munson

NEW ENGLISH LIBRARY
TIMES MIRROR

© 1975 New English Library

First published in Great Britain by New English Library, Barnard's Inn, Holborn, London, EC1 in 1975.

Printed and bound in Italy, by Fratelli Spada, Ciampino, Rome.
SBN 450 02180 7

Contents

Top: There are few good photographs of original Fokker *Eindeckers,* the first true fighter aircraft. This beautiful E.III replica was built by Doug Bianchi for use in the film *Crooks and Coronets*

This page:
Centre: D.H.2 'pusher' fighters of No 32 Squadron, Royal Flying Corps, at a front-line airfield in France. The D.H.2 was one of the types which ended the so-called Fokker Scourge in 1916

Bottom: Typical of the aircraft with which the RFC entered World War I was this totally-unarmed Blériot monoplane, not very different from the machine in which Louis Blériot had made the first cross-Channel flight five years earlier. Pilots were ordered to ram any Zeppelin they sighted *en route* from England to France. In fact, the Blériots would probably have been unable to climb fast enough or high enough to make this possible

Opposite page:
Left, top to bottom: The Fokker D.VII, perhaps the best fighter of 1918. It was really a cantilever biplane; the interplane struts were added only to give the German pilots greater confidence in its sturdy structure

The Vickers F.B.5 Gunbus was the first British aircraft designed specifically to carry a machine-gun. The 'pusher' layout permitted this to be mounted on the nose of the crew nacelle

Like the Gunbus, the D.H.2 carried its machine-gun at the front of its nacelle. This was the best position until the perfection of an interrupter gear made it possible to fire bullets between spinning propeller blades

Right, top: The Bristol F.2B Fighter was outstanding as a two-seat combat aircraft. Its agility enabled the pilot to make full use of a synchronised forward-firing machine-gun, to supplement the efforts of the gunner in the rear cockpit

Right, bottom: Using a Hucks starter to start the engine of a Sopwith Snipe, Britain's counterpart to the Fokker D.VII. By engaging its engine-driven shaft with a spigot on the aircraft's propeller boss, the Hucks starter offered an easier, safer alternative to hand swinging the 'prop'

GENESIS OF AIR COMBAT

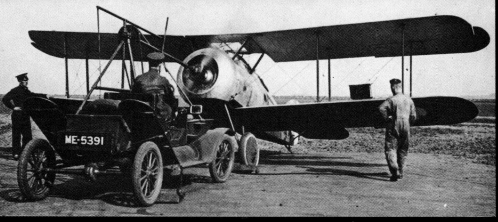

Although aviation in its broadest sense had already been used for military purposes for several decades before the Wright brothers' first aeroplane flights of 1903, it had in the main been confined to the use of free balloons for individual bombardment and tethered balloons for army reconnaissance. With the potential of controlled flight at the touch of a human hand, the military possibilities were recognised almost immediately.

Within a few years of its birth the aeroplane became the vehicle for experiments in gun and bomb carriage simultaneously in Great Britain, France, Germany and America. By 1911 several firing trials of machine-guns from aircraft pointed the path to one significant future for these frail structures; but, blinkered by centuries of inflexible ground strategy, the Army mind was capable of viewing the new means of locomotion only as an extension of the well-proven cavalry scout. With excusable finality, in view of the fragile nature of contemporary aircraft designs, most Army commanders regarded this new invention as a longer 'arm' of the infantry's primary requisite—reconnaissance. As such, the main characteristic sought in any military aeroplane was stability in flight, to provide a steady platform for the observer; any form of armament was considered unnecessary. Thus, at the outbreak of the European war in August 1914, few military aircraft were capable of carrying any form of bomb, while none was intended to carry a gun.

Despite these handicaps the first few weeks of the war saw attempts by a majority of pilots and observers to carry armament in their aircraft, albeit in most cases merely a Service rifle, pistol or private sporting gun. The concept of an aeroplane specifically designed for fighting was but dimly realised by a few individuals, with the result that in 1914 and early 1915 air units of the opposing air services were composed almost wholly of two-seat aircraft which were expected to fly in every role necessary for support of land operations. The few air casualties which occurred during the opening stages of the war were the outcome of sheer determination by individual crews; but on 1 April 1915 a new and deadly phase of air fighting was born. On that morning a lone French pilot, Roland Garros, took off in his Morane-Saulnier Type L monoplane on which he had fitted a crude device for air combat. After strapping a Hotchkiss machine-gun on the fuselage in front of his cockpit, firing forward along the line of flight, he had bolted steel wedges to the propeller in line with the gun barrel, to deflect any bullets that would otherwise strike the propeller blades. During his patrol Garros met a German Albatros observation two-seater and shot it down in flames.

Within a fortnight the Frenchman had claimed two more victims with his primitive and highly dangerous gun arrangement; but on 19 April he was forced to land behind the German lines after anti-aircraft fire had damaged his Morane. His gun device was salvaged from the partially-burned wreck of

This page, top to bottom:
No more than about 425 Fokker *Eindeckers* were built. Yet, because of their synchronised machine-guns, they almost shot the Allied air forces from the skies over France in 1915-16. The maximum take-off weight of the E.III version was 1,400 lb (635 kg)—about the same as the four air-to-air missiles carried as armament by some of its modern counterparts

An air mechanic handing photographic plates to the observer in an R.E.8 at an RFC aerodrome near Arras on 22 February 1918. Known affectionately as the 'Harry Tate', after a popular music hall artist of the time, the R.E.8 was the standard British photo-reconnaissance and artillery spotting aircraft in the last years of World War I

Bearing insignia typical of a machine flown by a German 'ace', this Albatros D.V scout belonged to Hauptmann Ritter von Schleich of Jasta 32, in 1917. Known as Germany's 'Black Knight', because he later flew an all-black D.Va, he was credited with 35 victories in air combat, and survived to become a leader of the new *Luftwaffe* in the 'thirties

Yet another of the fine replicas of World War I fighters built for use in films of the 'sixties was this Pfalz D.III. The genuine version was a contemporary of the Fokker D.VII and suffered unjustly from this, as German pilots were resentful when made to fly Pfalz D.IIIs and D.XIIs instead of the much-vaunted D.VII

Opposite page, top: This Fokker D.VII was photographed at Biggin Hill, England, in May 1919. Article IV of the Armistice Agreement signed by Germany had mentioned specifically that 'all machines of the D.VII type' were to be handed over to the Allies, the only time a specific aircraft type has ever been mentioned in such a document. Despite this, Anthony Fokker managed to smuggle about 120 more or less complete D.VIIs into his native Holland, where he re-started his business

Centre: Favourite mount of many of the British fighter pilots of World War I, the S.E.5a was a product of the Royal Aircraft Factory at Farnborough. Usual armament comprised a Lewis gun above the top wing, on a Foster mounting which enabled it to be slid down for reloading and for firing upward, and a forward-firing synchronised Vickers gun.

his aircraft and a copy was ordered immediately by the German high command for its own aircraft. Instead, three men of the Fokker aircraft company's staff produced a much-improved arrangement. They manufactured a mechanical interrupter gear which relied on the propeller itself to operate a machine-gun's firing mechanism, thus preventing the gun from firing when a blade aligned with the gun barrel. The gear was fitted to a Fokker M.5K monoplane scout and on 1 July 1915 Leutnant Kurt Wintgens used the new gun gear to destroy a French Morane. His victory was soon repeated by other Fokker pilots, including Oswald Boelcke, Max Immelmann and Max Mülzer. It was the start of what came to be called the 'Fokker Scourge', when the British and French flying services suffered rapidly increasing losses to the agile *Eindeckers*.

With no comparable gun gear immediately available, Allied designers were forced to compromise by producing aircraft with machine-guns mounted to fire outside the propeller arc on normal 'tractor' aircraft, as in the case of the French Nieuport scouts. A second answer to the problem was exemplified by the Vickers F.B.5 (the first British aircraft built specifically for fighting duties), de Havilland D.H.2 scout and the curiously efficient F.E.2b two-seater. All three of these were of the 'pusher' type, with both crew and machine-gun placed in front of the engine. Only the F.B.5s were in France in 1915, equipping No. 11 Squadron RFC, the first British unit formed for a fighting role. In February 1916, the D.H.2-equipped 24 Squadron arrived on the Western Front, commanded by Major Lanoe Hawker, VC, DSO, the RFC's first 'fighting' ace; and in the following month 25 Squadron (F.E.2bs) and 27 Squadron (Martinsyde G.100s) moved to France. Meanwhile, between the autumn of 1915 and early 1916 the Fokker scourge spread like a blight across the fighting areas above the Western Front. The almost defenceless Allied reconnaissance machines were no match for an armed Fokker scout, not least because their once-all-important stability robbed them of the ability to manoeuvre quickly when attacked.

Once the new fighters of British and French units got into their stride in the summer of 1916, the Fokker menace was soon abated and for a very brief period the Allies regained aerial supremacy. But their minor triumph was short-lived, for in late 1916 new fighting machines began to appear in German *Jagdstaffeln* (literally, Hunting Squadrons)—the Albatros D.I and D.II scouts and the Halberstadt D. series.

Of streamlined shape, with a plywood-skinned fuselage, the Albatros carried twin synchronised machine-guns firing through the propeller arc—an armament arrangement which was to become classic in most fighter aircraft for the remainder of the war and, indeed, for nearly twenty years after. Almost immediately the German Imperial Air Service regained its former air supremacy and it was not until the following spring that the Allies began receiving comparable aircraft types. Of these new designs,

Even after fighters became, generally, tractor-engined, Lewis-gunners still manned open gun positions in the nose of bombers like this Handley Page O/400 of September 1918

the most significant were the Bristol F.2B two-seat fighter, and the S.E.5 and Sopwith Camel scouts, all with synchronised machine-guns.

In many ways the Camel epitomised the World War I fighting machine. Armed with twin Vickers guns and powered by a rotary engine, it was a thoroughly unstable flying machine with the manoeuvrability of a will-o'-the-wisp, and so ideal for the lightning cut-and-thrust of 1917-18 air combat. Its highly unstable qualities, the antithesis of 1914 design ideals, made the little Sopwith one of the supreme dogfighters of the war, only equalled perhaps by the notorious Fokker Dr.I triplane scout which began to equip German units in late 1917.

During 1917 and 1918, fighter design showed an astonishing improvement over the fragile aircraft used on operations at the start of the conflict. Scouts were built and flown with four and even six machine-guns; while the French experimented with heavier-calibre shell guns of up to 37 mm from an early date. Primitive electrically-ignited rockets were employed with limited success, while on the German side experiments produced functional aerial cannon and even multi-barrel machine-guns—forerunners of the present-day weapons in international use.

In design, the 1918 scouts showed the influence of lessons learned in the hard school of combat experience over nearly four years of war. Engines, though still imperfect, were in the 150-185 hp range, giving speeds of over 100 mph (161 km/h) in normal flight. By that year Germany had produced her most successful fighting aeroplane of the war, the Fokker D.VII. With a basic structure of welded steel tubing, fabric covered, and capable of speeds in excess of 125 mph (201 km/h) at heights above 15,000 feet (4,570 m), the D.VII eventually equipped the bulk of *Jagdstaffeln* before the Armistice. Its nearest competitor in performance was a successor to the waspish Camel, the Sopwith Snipe, which was beginning to re-equip RAF units during the final weeks of hostilities.

With the cessation of fighting in November 1918, the impetus given to aircraft designers by the incessant demands of war was allowed to die away. It had been an heroic era which produced legendary names in military aviation history. Aircrews had fought and died two and three miles high over the muddied trenches, without benefit of oxygen, wireless communication, parachutes or heated cockpits. Tactics had been empirical, as were the ever-changing design requirements of the tiny aircraft in which such men had flown. But the tradition carved out by crews and aircraft proved to be a rock foundation for succeeding generations of men and machines.

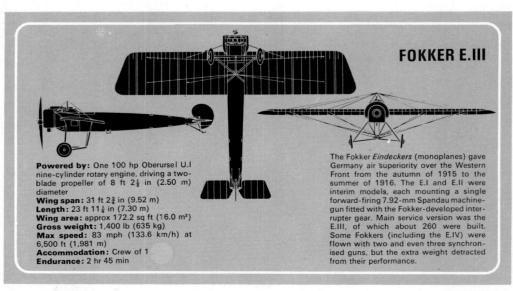

FOKKER E.III

Powered by: One 100 hp Oberursel U.I nine-cylinder rotary engine, driving a two-blade propeller of 8 ft 2½ in (2.50 m) diameter
Wing span: 31 ft 2¾ in (9.52 m)
Length: 23 ft 11¼ in (7.30 m)
Wing area: approx 172.2 sq ft (16.0 m²)
Gross weight: 1,400 lb (635 kg)
Max speed: 83 mph (133.6 km/h) at 6,500 ft (1,981 m)
Accommodation: Crew of 1
Endurance: 2 hr 45 min

The Fokker *Eindeckers* (monoplanes) gave Germany air superiority over the Western Front from the autumn of 1915 to the summer of 1916. The E.I and E.II were interim models, each mounting a single forward-firing 7.92-mm Spandau machine-gun fitted with the Fokker-developed interrupter gear. Main service version was the E.III, of which about 260 were built. Some Fokkers (including the E.IV) were flown with two and even three synchronised guns, but the extra weight detracted from their performance.

Above: This Sopwith Pup is still flown regularly for the delight of visitors to the Shuttleworth Collection of historical aircraft at Old Warden aerodrome in Bedfordshire. It was built just after World War I as a Dove, civilian counterpart of the Pup. After an accident, it was converted into a Pup and still reminds both pilots and spectators why this type was regarded by many as the finest flying machine ever built

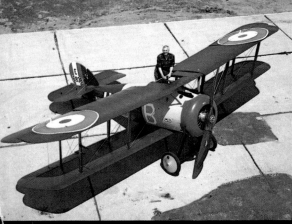

Extreme left: Known as 'The Eagle of Lille' Max Immelmann was the great exponent of the Fokker *Eindecker*. After claiming 15 victories in air combat, he was lost in action. German accounts attributed his death to a technical failure of his aircraft; the RFC claimed that he fell to the guns of Corporal Waller in an F.E.2b fighter

Centre, top: Judged by many to be the finest World War I aeroplane still flying in the USA, this Sopwith Snipe bears no visible scars of the Hollywood studio fire in which it was once severely damaged. Built in 1918, it still has its original 230-hp Bentley B.R.2 rotary engine.

Centre, bottom: The remains of Immelmann's Fokker monoplane, in which he died on 18 June 1916. It was stated officially that his interrupter gear had failed, causing the engine to 'run away' and break up the airframe after the propeller had been shot away. Immelmann's death symbolised the end of the Fokker's brief reign of supremacy

Left, top to bottom:
Hauptmann Ritter von Tutschek (27 victories) preparing to take off in his Fokker Dr.I triplane in March 1918. An aircraft of this type was the favourite mount of Germany's 'ace of aces', Manfred von Richthofen

Morane-Saulnier Type N scout of the Royal Flying Corps. One of many fine types acquired from French production, the Type N had steel deflector plates fitted to its propeller blades to kick aside any bullets from the machine-gun that would otherwise have hit them

Very few combat aircraft of Russian design served in World War I, except for Sikorsky's great Ilya Mourometz bombers. However, a few Sikorsky S-20s, like this one, reached front-line squadrons and are said to have been capable of 118 mph (190 km/h) on the power of a 110-hp Le Rhône engine

the start of air bombing

In 1670 Father Francesco de Lana-Terzi wrote a treatise on the feasibility of building an 'aerial ship'. Utterly convinced of such a possibility, the worthy cleric also foresaw clearly a military application for such a vehicle as a weapon of bombardment, being probably the first man to do so. It was to be two and a half centuries before his dire prophecy became reality.

The first known occasion of bombs being dropped from an aeroplane in war operations took place on 1 November 1911, during the Italo-Turkish conflict in Libya. On that date Second Lieutenant Guilio Gavotti of the Italian Air Flotilla threw four 4.4-lb (2-kg) 'Cipelli' grenades from his aircraft on to enemy troops at Taguira Oasis and Ain Zara. With eleven pilots flying a mixed collection of nine aircraft, Gavotti and his comrades exploited their air bombing technique to such good effect that a correspondent attached to the Turkish Army commented: 'This war has shown clearly that air navigation (sic) provides a terrible means of destruction. These new weapons are destined to revolutionise modern strategy and tactics'. His visionary remarks made little impact on contemporary military minds. Even the Wright brothers had optimistically proclaimed their invention as 'a certain means of ending war', while few nations considered the aeroplane as other than a passing fad, or at best a useful, if limited, adjunct to the armies.

The notion of utilising aeroplanes for bombing was by no means neglected entirely. In the USA as early as January 1910 serious trials of releasing a 'war load' were carried out, although the lethal load on the first occasion was merely three 2-lb (0.9 kg) sandbags. Almost exactly one year later the first test involving a live explosive bomb was completed with some success. In Britain, too, thought had been given to such employment of aircraft. By 1912 various experimental flights had begun to explore the possibilities of air bombing, notably by individual naval officers such as Charles Rumsey Samson and Robert Clark-Hall. Their experiences were largely ignored by both Admiralty and War Office, and on the outbreak of war with Germany in 1914 Britain's only stockpile of true aerial bombs comprised twenty-six 20-lb (9-kg) Hales bombs stored at Eastchurch on the Isle of Sheppey. All were intended to be released by hand, there being no such thing as a bomb carrier and very few aircraft capable of bearing a bomb load in Service use at that time.

France, with slightly superior foresight, had already decided that aerial bombardment was practical and began the war relatively well-equipped with several squadrons of Voisin 'pusher' bombers. Within a few weeks of hostilities beginning, these sturdy aircraft had carried out a series of short-range attacks against German targets behind the front lines. In Germany, too, the strategic possibilities of air power had been recognised early. With an airship fleet and a comparatively large aeroplane service, Germany already had plans for an aerial attack on England. Brain-child of an elderly Army Major, Wilhelm Siegert, this was to include the bombing of cities and industrial centres in south-east England and thus could be regarded as the true genesis of strategic air bombing.

Above, left: In the early days of the 1914-18 War, bombs were usually dropped by hand. This photograph shows an RNAS officer about to drop a bomb from the control car of an airship in this manner

Above, right: Loading a standard 112-lb (50-kg) bomb on the starboard wing rack of a D.H.4 of No 27 Squadron, RFC, in February 1918.

Opposite page:
Top left: This 230-lb (104-kg) bomb was also delivered by a D.H.4 of No 27 Squadron

Top right: At the outbreak of war, aeroplanes were still regarded by the armies of the world as novelties, useful only for reconnaissance. This unarmed Maurice Farman was typical of French military aircraft of the period

Centre right: This photograph of the unfortunate end of a Sopwith 1½-Strutter of No 5 Wing, RNAS, is interesting in that it shows clearly the 'bomb cell' in the fuselage, between the lower wings

Right: One of the North Sea class of non-rigid airships which put in fine service with the RNAS in World War 1

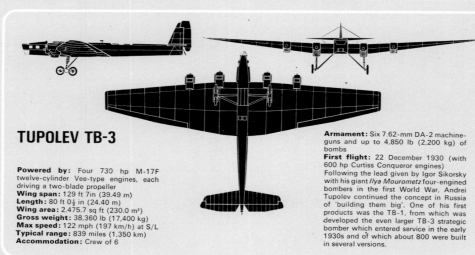

TUPOLEV TB-3

Powered by: Four 730 hp M-17F twelve-cylinder Vee-type engines, each driving a two-blade propeller
Wing span: 129 ft 7in (39.49 m)
Length: 80 ft 0½ in (24.40 m)
Wing area: 2,475.7 sq ft (230.0 m²)
Gross weight: 38,360 lb (17,400 kg)
Max speed: 122 mph (197 km/h) at S/L
Typical range: 839 miles (1,350 km)
Accommodation: Crew of 6

Armament: Six 7.62-mm DA-2 machine-guns and up to 4,850 lb (2,200 kg) of bombs
First flight: 22 December 1930 (with 600 hp Curtiss Conqueror engines)
Following the lead given by Igor Sikorsky with his giant *Ilya Mourometz* four-engined bombers in the first World War, Andrei Tupolev continued the concept in Russia of 'building them big'. One of his first products was the TB-1, from which was developed the even larger TB-3 strategic bomber which entered service in the early 1930s and of which about 800 were built in several versions.

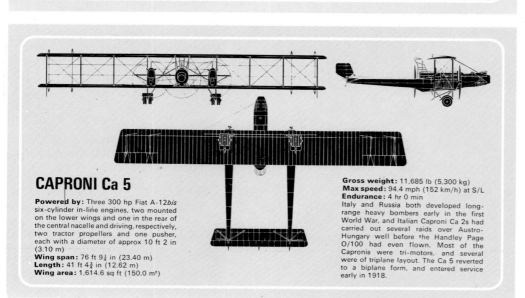

CAPRONI Ca 5

Powered by: Three 300 hp Fiat A-12*bis* six-cylinder in-line engines, two mounted on the lower wings and one in the rear of the central nacelle and driving, respectively, two tractor propellers and one pusher, each with a diameter of approx 10 ft 2 in (3.10 m)
Wing span: 76 ft 9¼ in (23.40 m)
Length: 41 ft 4¾ in (12.62 m)
Wing area: 1,614.6 sq ft (150.0 m²)

Gross weight: 11,685 lb (5,300 kg)
Max speed: 94.4 mph (152 km/h) at S/L
Endurance: 4 hr 0 min
Italy and Russia both developed long-range heavy bombers early in the first World War, and Italian Caproni Ca 2s had carried out several raids over Austro-Hungary well before the Handley Page O/100 had even flown. Most of the Capronis were tri-motors, and several were of triplane layout. The Ca 5 reverted to a biplane form, and entered service early in 1918.

Top, left: Big bombers are nothing new in Russia. One of Igor Sikorsky's four-engined *Ilya Mourometz* bombers was used for tests with this 920-lb (417-kg) weapon. The figure 1 identifies Sikorsky; No 3 is General Michael Vladimirovich Shidlowsky, who commanded the 'Squadron of Flying Ships'

Top right: An *Ilya Mourometz* in flight. Of 73 built, about half were used at the front; only one was shot down over enemy territory

This page, centre: The IM-G3 version of the *Ilya Mourometz* had two 220-hp Renault inner engines and two 150-hp RBZ-6 outers. It had defensive gun positions in nose and tail, and a further machine-gun which could fire upward or downward from inside the fuselage. Bomb-load was 2,000 lb (907 kg)

Above: 'One night's rations'. Preparing 112-lb bombs for a night raid by No 149 Squadron, RAF, equipped with F.E.2bs, on 18 July 1918

Opposite page, top: Caproni's big Ca 42 three-engined triplane could carry up to 3,910 lb (1,775 kg) of bombs in the pannier on its bottom wing. Spanning nearly 100 ft (30 m), it had a maximum speed of 87 mph (140 km/h) and could fly for seven hours

Right: First used in February 1918, the 1,650 lb (748 kg) 'Minor' was the largest bomb dropped by British Handley Page O/400s. A 3,300-pounder, evolved for the four-engined HP V/1500, was never used operationally

The war soon accelerated progress in this field of operations. Within the first few months, individual pilots of the Royal Naval Air Service had undertaken bombing sorties against such targets as Zeppelin sheds and supply depots. The aircraft used were lightly loaded and woefully under-powered, but the morale value of their limited successes encouraged officialdom to regard the 'new' weapon seriously. Until late 1915, the use of bomb-carrying aircraft was still restricted mainly to tactical support of land operations; but before the year was out the Allied commanders had agreed to the formation of a unit for purely strategic operations. This unit, No 3 Wing RNAS, came into being by July 1916 equipped with Sopwith 1½-Strutter single-engined aircraft of limited range and light bomb load. The Wing's career was comparatively short, the aircraft being diverted to supply under-strength RFC and RNAS squadrons along the Western Front by June 1917.

While able to lay claim to being the first strategic bomber unit, No 3 Wing RNAS was by no means the first formation created specifically for bombing operations. Apart from the French Voisin *escadrilles* already mentioned, Russia possessed a squadron of giant four-engined *Ilya Mourometz* aircraft, which made its first raid against a target in Poland on 15 February 1915; and in Italy Caproni three-engined bombers had flown their first long-range sorties on 20 August 1915.

Despite the hurried dispersal of No 3

Wing, the principle of strategic bombing was not abandoned by Britain, being reborn with the formation of the 41st Wing, Royal Flying Corps, in 1917. In addition to two squadrons equipped with F.E.2b and D.H.4 aircraft, the Wing employed a significant new design, the twin-engined Handley Page O/100. Conceived in 1914, this behemoth, with a wing span of 100 feet (30.48 m), was capable of lifting an 1,800-lb (816-kg) load over a range of at least 200 miles (322 km). With the improved O/400, it was the fore-runner of several generations of British heavy bombers during the succeeding forty years. Beginning operations in October 1917, the Wing was strengthened by two additional squadrons in May 1918, by which time its title had become VIII Brigade, Royal Air Force. Primary targets were German cities, which were attacked by day and night, and in June 1918 VIII Brigade became the nucleus of a completely new formation, the Independent Force, RAF.

While the principle behind the creation of such a force was sound, its birth was due in no small measure to a simple, primitive desire for retaliation rather than any visionary concept of strategy. Due to the increasing number of bombing raids flown against Britain by the German Zeppelins (and, by 1917, Gotha bombers), British public opinion expressed a wish for ven-geance. The Gotha raids began on 25 May 1917 and were undertaken by a group of four squadrons formed specially for the purpose of raiding the United Kingdom

This page:

Top: A Handley Page O/400 bomber of No 207 Squadron, RAF, flying over the Occupation Zone of Germany in May 1919

Left: This 1,650-pounder was dropped from an HP O/400 of No 207 Squadron on Le Cateau railway station during the night of 13/14 September 1918

Above: Powered by two 360 hp Rolls-Royce Eagle engines, the Handley Page O/400 had a top speed of 97.5 mph (157 km/h). About 400 were delivered to the British Services before the Armistice

Opposite page, top: Servicing an O/400 at Dunkirk in 1918. Its heavy defensive armament included twin guns in the nose and two more above the fuselage amidships. A fifth gun fired rearward and downward through the bottom of the fuselage

centre: One of the fine three-engined Caproni biplanes with which Italy pioneered long-range strategic bombing across the Alps in 1915-18

bottom: British bombs of 1914-18. From left to right: 16-lb (7.25-kg) incendiary, 65-lb (29.5-kg) high-explosive, 112-lb (50-kg) RL (Royal Laboratory), 100-lb (45-kg) RL and 230-lb (104-kg) RFC Mk 3. Those on the shelf at rear include 25-lb (11.3-kg) Coopers

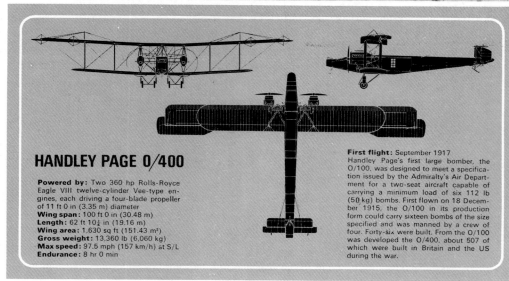

HANDLEY PAGE O/400

Powered by: Two 360 hp Rolls-Royce Eagle VIII twelve-cylinder Vee-type engines, each driving a four-blade propeller of 11 ft 0 in (3.35 m) diameter
Wing span: 100 ft 0 in (30.48 m)
Length: 62 ft 10¼ in (19.16 m)
Wing area: 1,630 sq ft (151.43 m²)
Gross weight: 13,360 lb (6,060 kg)
Max speed: 97.5 mph (157 km/h) at S/L
Endurance: 8 hr 0 min

First flight: September 1917
Handley Page's first large bomber, the O/100, was designed to meet a specification issued by the Admiralty's Air Department for a two-seat aircraft capable of carrying a minimum load of six 112 lb (50 kg) bombs. First flown on 18 December 1915, the O/100 in its production form could carry sixteen bombs of the size specified and was manned by a crew of four. Forty-six were built. From the O/100 was developed the O/400, about 507 of which were built in Britain and the US during the war.

from bases in Belgium. In pursuance of the policy first propounded by Siegert in 1914, this group, titled *Kampfgeschwader Nr 3* (the 'England Squadron') was equipped initially with twin-engined Gotha bombers capable of reaching most south-eastern counties of England, including London, with a useful bomb load. Later additional designs included the mammoth *Riesenflugzeug* or 'Giant' aircraft, and their depredations continued for almost exactly one year, until May 1918.

Within a month of the Gothas' final raid the Independent Force came into being under the command of Sir Hugh Trenchard. Initially it comprised units of the defunct VIII Brigade, but by September 1918 a further five squadrons had been added to its strength. The new Force's terms of reference included 'an extended and sustained bombing offensive against German munition industries'. In practical terms the IF's offensive produced a lowering of German civilian morale twenty times greater than the material damage accomplished. It was this latter effect, undoubtedly ,which led to the formation of No 27 Group, RAF, a tiny collection of three new squadrons which were due to equip with Handley Page V/1500 bombers—four-engined developments of the well-proven O/400s. These 'Super-Handleys' were expected to reach and devastate Berlin, the German capital city, with loads of up to 3,400 lb (1,542 kg) —although it is open to speculation whether the V/1500s would have been capable of such sorties. The opportunity for practice never came, for the Armistice of November 1918 intervened.

The four years of war had seen bombing aircraft develop from frail 80-hp craft, whose pilots dispensed hand grenades and 20-lb (9-kg) bombs by hand, to giant aircraft spanning over 100 ft (30.48 m), twin- and four-engined and capable of transporting loads of up to nearly 4,000 lb (1,814 kg) weight over relatively long ranges with reasonable accuracy. And, most important, the first principles of strategic air policy had taken root in the more receptive military minds of all nations. Within two decades, the consequences were to bring devastating results.

Left: One of the main operational duties of the Royal Navy's Sopwith Camel fighters was to intercept German Zeppelins over the North Sea, when the airships shadowed or attacked Allied naval forces. Many were flown from wooden platforms built over the swivelling gun turrets of warships, as shown here

Centre: Last of the series of Short seaplanes used by the RNAS and RAF in World War 1, the Short 320 derived its name from the fact that it was powered by a 320-hp Sunbeam Cossack engine. Post-war, torpedo-bombing duties were taken over increasingly by carrier-based landplanes

HOW THE AEROPLANE WENT TO SEA

A mere decade after the Wright brothers had demonstrated, in their own words, 'that the age of the flying machine had come at last', the first World War gave an impetus to the development of the aeroplane which established its place firmly in the armouries of the nations. When the war started in 1914, however, the roles which could be played by the rudimentary machines of the period was far from clear. Whilst a handful of forward-thinking individuals grasped the significance of the aeroplane for military duties, to the majority it was still a novelty and little more than a frivolous toy.

Experiments often had to be conducted in the face of official apathy and public derision. The efforts to exploit the aeroplane as an adjunct to the operations of the Royal Navy were no exception. Interest in sea-flying had grown through the efforts of Fabre and Curtiss in 1910, and before the end of that year Ely in America had made the world's first take-off from a ship, the USS *Birmingham*. By 1911, it was becoming clear that the aeroplane might have a role for fleet reconnaissance and coastal patrol, and in the face of a somewhat reluctant Admiralty, Royal Navy aviators pressed ahead with experiments to see how ships and aeroplanes could work together.

Early in 1911, in America, Ely landed his Curtiss biplane on the *Pennsylvania*, which, like the *Birmingham* two months before, had a platform constructed for the purpose. During both flights, however, the ship was moored at the dockside. A similar take-off was made for the first time in Britain a year later, on 10 January 1912, by Lieut Charles Samson in a Short S.27 from a deck erected on HMS *Africa*. Thereafter, Samson played

Left: At the beginning of World War 1, only seaplanes operated from the primitive carriers of the day. They had to be lowered over the side by crane, to take off from the sea, with the result that their floats broke up if the water was rough. By the end of the war, even the comparatively 'hot' Sopwith Camel was able to operate safely from the first genuine carriers of the Royal Navy

Right: In the days before deck lifts were invented, great care had to be taken when passing aircraft by crane through the hatchway leading to the below-deck hangar on HMS *Furious*. Fortunately, the Sopwith Pup was quite small. Later types needed folding wings, and the naval 2F.1 Camel had a detachable rear fuselage

Centre: For a period during, and immediately after, World War 1 aircraft like this Sopwith 1½-Strutter were operated from RN carriers with skid landing gear. The rails on the ship's deck helped to keep the aircraft on a straight course

a prominent role in developing the Royal Navy's flying branch. However, several years were to elapse before deck flying became a practical possibility.

In 1914, responsibility for the air defence of Great Britain was vested in the Royal Naval Air Service, adding to its duties of fleet reconnaissance and coastal patrol. Thus, the RNAS operated landplanes from land bases from the start of the war—and this provided the Service with experience in aerial defence which was later applied with good effect to its ship-based operations.

For coastal patrols, a mixture of landplanes and seaplanes was operated from shore bases such as that at Great Yarmouth. Guns and bombs were soon added to these aeroplanes—the majority were Short biplanes—making them the forerunners of today's shore-based maritime reconnaissance types such as the Nimrod, Orion and Atlantic.

Fleet reconnaissance, on the other hand, implied operation of the aircraft wherever ships of the fleet sailed. Samson's 1912 flight from the *Africa*, on a pontoon-equipped Short biplane, led to the introduction of seaplane carriers by the Royal Navy. Hastily converted merchantmen had wooden platforms erected over the bows, from which seaplanes could be launched (with the aid of a wheeled trolley) or could be lifted over the side to take off conventionally from the open sea. At the end of a mission, the seaplane would land alongside the carrier to be retrieved by crane.

Earliest of the ships so converted were the cross-Channel steamers *Empress*, *Engadine* and *Riviera*, each carrying four seaplanes, and the Cunarder *Campania*, which could carry ten seaplanes. Other conversions followed, including the cross-Channel *Manxman*, *Ben-My-Chree* and *Vindex*, plus the *Ark Royal*, a merchantman converted during construction.

On Christmas Day, 1914, a force of seven Short seaplanes from the *Empress*, *Engadine* and *Riviera* was launched from a position 12 miles (20 km) north of Heligoland to attack the German Zeppelin sheds at Cuxhaven. The raid was ineffective, due primarily to poor weather, but was the

Right: The man who proved that landplanes could be landed on a moving ship, as well as flown off, was Squadron Commander E H Dunning. This historic photograph shows him making his first, successful touch-down on the forward deck of HMS *Furious*, on 2 August 1917. As soon as he was on deck, colleagues grabbed the little aeroplane to prevent it from lifting again. Dunning was killed when he tried to repeat the experiment unaided

first demonstration of the way in which the range of offensive aircraft could be increased by operating them from ships. The deterrent value of this development was shown when the German Navy moved a number of its ships from the Channel ports to the Baltic, to avoid further attack.

Another demonstration of the growing importance of aeroplanes in naval operations came in 1915, in the Dardanelles campaign. Seaplanes from HMS *Ark Royal* began operating on 17 February 1915, spotting for the guns of the fleet. In August, the *Ben-My-Chree* arrived with two Short 184s, each able to carry a 14-inch (355 mm) torpedo. On 12 August a direct hit on a Turkish merchant vessel was claimed for a torpedo dropped by one of these aircraft.

Flying from the seaplane carriers, open water or coastal bases, seaplanes of the Royal Navy played a significant role throughout the war, and their evolution was matched by similar work in France and Germany. Meanwhile, the RNAS continued experiments to improve the technique of operating aircraft from ships, and this was to give Britain a clear lead by 1918 in the development of aircraft carriers in the modern sense of the term. The primary objective of the experiments was to permit the operation of wheeled aeroplanes from ships, which would not then have to heave-to in order to launch and recover their seaplanes.

An early experiment was made on 3 November 1915, when Flt Sub-Lt H F Towler took off in a Bristol Scout from the deck of the seaplane carrier *Vindex*, subsequently ditching alongside the ship with the aid of flotation bags. Further impetus was given to these developments by the

growth of German Zeppelin operations, which could be combated only by fighters of considerably higher performance than the seaplanes in use by the RNAS. Early in 1917, both the *Campania* and *Manxman* were issued with Pup fighters, after Flt-Cdr F J Rutland had shown that this Sopwith biplane could be flown easily off the seaplane decks on these ships. By refining flying techniques, Rutland went on to demonstrate that the Pup could take off after a 15 ft (4.6 m) run at a speed of about 23 mph (37 km/h).

As a result of this development, a total of 22 British light cruisers, starting with HMS *Yarmouth*, were fitted with 20-ft (6.1-m) flying-off platforms and issued with fighters. On 21 August 1917, a Pup launched by the *Yarmouth* and flown by Flt Sub-Lt B A Smart intercepted and shot down the Zeppelin L.23. To overcome the objection that the ships had to turn into wind to launch their aircraft, Rutland evolved a technique for flying off platforms attached to the swivelling gun turrets of battle cruisers, which then adopted two fighters each as standard equipment.

An alternative scheme was evolved in 1918 by Charles Samson (by this time a Colonel) in which a fighter was towed on a 40 ft (12.2-m) barge behind destroyers or other warships. The barge had a rudimentary 'flight deck' from which the fighter could rise almost vertically when being towed at speed into wind. Using this technique, Flt Sub-Lt Stuart Culley was launched in a Sopwith Camel, towed behind the destroyer HMS *Redoubt*, off the Dutch coast on 11 August 1918 to intercept the Zeppelin L.53. This he did at the extreme ceiling of his aircraft, above 18,000 ft

This page, top left: When the French Navy needed more seaplanes desperately at the start of World War 1, a young engineer named Alphonse Tellier was engaged to design a suitable machine. This led, in 1917, to the production of 96 Tellier T.3 two-seat bomber flying-boats and 55 T.C.6s, armed with a 47-mm cannon. This later Tellier flying-boat had three 350-hp engines, and a 75-mm gun in the nose

Above: HMS *Furious* at the time when she had a completely clear flight deck. The smoke plume streaming back from the bows indicated when the ship was sailing dead into wind, so that flying off could begin

Top right: The serial number on the rudder of this prototype led to production models being known as Short 184s. One of them became the first aircraft ever to sink an enemy ship by torpedo, during the Dardanelles campaign. Another was the only aeroplane to take part in the naval Battle of Jutland

Opposite page, top right: America's first aircraft carrier, the USS *Langley*, was a converted collier. Her first squadron was equipped with Vought VE-7SF single-seat fighters. In one of these, Lt V C Griffin made the first-ever take-off from a US Navy carrier on 17 October 1922

Centre: The US Navy acquired a total of 22 Sopwith 1½-Strutters. Like the Royal Navy, it tried operating the type from a platform built over the gun turret of a warship

Bottom: HMS *Argus*, known in the Royal Navy as the 'flat iron' for obvious reasons, survived in combat use into World War 2. This photograph shows her operating with Seafires, off the North African coast, despite the fact that these fighters had a top speed three times as great as that of the fastest combat aircraft of 1918, when the ship was first commissioned

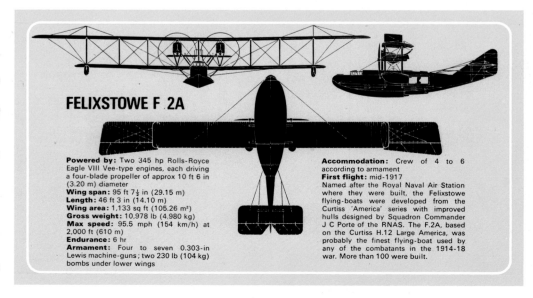

FELIXSTOWE F.2A

Powered by: Two 345 hp Rolls-Royce Eagle VIII Vee-type engines, each driving a four-blade propeller of approx 10 ft 6 in (3.20 m) diameter
Wing span: 95 ft 7½ in (29.15 m)
Length: 46 ft 3 in (14.10 m)
Wing area: 1,133 sq ft (105.26 m²)
Gross weight: 10,978 lb (4,980 kg)
Max speed: 95.5 mph (154 km/h) at 2,000 ft (610 m)
Endurance: 6 hr
Armament: Four to seven 0.303-in Lewis machine-guns; two 230 lb (104 kg) bombs under lower wings

Accommodation: Crew of 4 to 6 according to armament
First flight: mid-1917
Named after the Royal Naval Air Station where they were built, the Felixstowe flying-boats were developed from the Curtiss 'America' series with improved hulls designed by Squadron Commander J C Porte of the RNAS. The F.2A, based on the Curtiss H.12 Large America, was probably the finest flying-boat used by any of the combatants in the 1914-18 war. More than 100 were built.

(5,500 m); standing the Camel on its tail, he fired a short but fatal burst into the Zeppelin before stalling.

None of these techniques allowed the aircraft to land back on the ship which launched them, although provision was made for them to be ditched and hoisted back on board—provided the ship could be found at the end of the flight. The final stage, therefore, was to find a means of landing on deck. The first hair-raising experiments were made in August 1917 on board HMS *Furious*, a light battle cruiser converted during construction to carry seaplanes and wheeled aeroplanes, which were launched from a flying-off deck 228 ft (70 m) long ahead of the bridge structure.

Combining a ship speed of about 21 knots and a wind speed of 25 knots or more, the airflow over the flight deck could match the landing speed of the Sopwith Pup. Sqdn Cdr E H Dunning took advantage of this to show how the aircraft could be landed-on. Flying up alongside the *Furious*, he side-slipped in ahead of the bridge and virtually hovered over the deck while colleagues grabbed the aircraft as he cut the throttle. A successful landing—the first on board a warship under way—was made on 2 August 1917. Less than a week later Dunning was killed in a further attempt.

In March 1918, the final step towards the true aircraft carrier was taken with the provision of a landing deck on *Furious*, aft of the bridge structure. The eddies round this structure and the exhaust from the funnel made landing on this deck extremely hazardous, but all the ingredients of the true aircraft carrier had now been provided and the aeroplane was able to go to sea without losing its operational effectiveness.

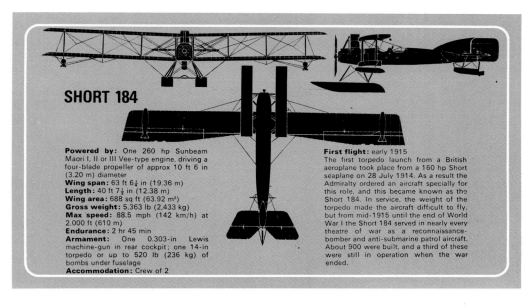

SHORT 184

Powered by: One 260 hp Sunbeam Maori I, II or III Vee-type engine, driving a four-blade propeller of approx 10 ft 6 in (3.20 m) diameter
Wing span: 63 ft 6¼ in (19.36 m)
Length: 40 ft 7½ in (12.38 m)
Wing area: 688 sq ft (63.92 m²)
Gross weight: 5,363 lb (2,433 kg)
Max speed: 88.5 mph (142 km/h) at 2,000 ft (610 m)
Endurance: 2 hr 45 min
Armament: One 0.303-in Lewis machine-gun in rear cockpit; one 14-in torpedo or up to 520 lb (236 kg) of bombs under fuselage
Accommodation: Crew of 2

First flight: early 1915
The first torpedo launch from a British aeroplane took place from a 160 hp Short seaplane on 28 July 1914. As a result the Admiralty ordered an aircraft specially for this role, and this became known as the Short 184. In service, the weight of the torpedo made the aircraft difficult to fly, but from mid-1915 until the end of World War I the Short 184 served in nearly every theatre of war as a reconnaissance-bomber and anti-submarine patrol aircraft. About 900 were built, and a third of these were still in operation when the war ended.

Top: The Westland Wapiti epitomises the 'general purpose' type of aircraft used for air control. To keep costs to a minimum it used as many existing D.H.9A components as possible including, originally, complete 'Ninak' wings

Left: The Vickers Victoria was a 22-passenger troop transport based on the Virginia bomber. Eight Victorias of No 70 Squadron spearheaded the famous airlift from Kabul, which evacuated 586 civilians, including King Inyatullah of Afghanistan and his family, during the rebellion of 1928-29

Bottom left: Powered like the Victoria Mk VI with Pegasus engines, the Valentia could be distinguished by its tail-wheel which replaced the tail-skid of the earlier type. It served for ten years from 1934, in the Middle East and India

Above: Workhorse of the air control squadrons was the D.H.9A. After extremely effective daylight bombing of German targets in the last few months of the first World War, this two-seater fought the Bolsheviks in Russia and dissident tribesmen everywhere from Aden and Iraq to the North-West Frontier of India

Centre right: The city of Mosul, in Iraq, was just one of the places kept in a state of relative peace by the air control squadrons. By maintaining the deterrent threat of bombing trouble-makers, aircraft like this Wapiti avoided the bloodshed on both sides that had always seemed inevitable when land forces were used

Bottom right: First of the famous series of Caproni 'colonial' bombers produced for the Italian Air Force in the inter-war years was the Ca 73. Layout was unusual, as the upper wing had a smaller span than the lower one, and the two 400 hp Lorraine engines were slung between them in a tandem 'power egg'

Far right: The Sopwith Snipe single-seat fighter was another combat aircraft of first World War vintage which was employed for many years on air control duties. These Snipes of No 1 Squadron were photographed near Baghdad in 1926

Air Control

AS EARLY AS 1911-12, during the Italo-Turkish War in Tripolitania, the aeroplane had demonstrated its potential for bombing, reconnaissance and leaflet-dropping. Thus it was first applied as an instrument of colonial warfare, an application which was to be emphasised to the point of exercising primary, and even absolute, air control in later years. The story of how this came about relates firstly to the RAF, and the philosophy behind such operations was once set out by an officer of that Service in these terms:

'Air control is the use of aircraft as the primary arm to support the political administration of an undeveloped country for the purpose of creating or restoring law and order. Aircraft usually act in co-operation with land forces, which fill some ancillary, but, nevertheless, important role—the securing, for instance, of the base for police purposes, or the pushing home of advantages gained by the air arm. Mountain, desert, marsh and swamp offer no obstruction to aircraft, which, ignoring such barriers, can penetrate to the source of trouble —right to the leader's fortress—within a few hours of its discovery. Against this arm uncivilised people are almost helpless, for they have practically no means of retaliation. Much of the effectiveness of air control depends, however, on good intelligence, which gives an intimate knowledge of the habits, mentality and pulse of the people, and enables pressure to be applied and confined at the centre of unrest. . . . Air operations are planned not to spread death and suffering, but to wear down the tribesman's morale, dislocate his normal life and thus make his existence wretched and intolerable.'

These plainly enunciated principles were carried into effect frequently in the years between the wars—years when RAF overseas operations were considerably more extensive than is commonly supposed, although it was seldom necessary to send home-based squadrons abroad to supplement those already there. Another point which is not, perhaps, widely enough appreciated is that almost every RAF officer and man with more than five years in uniform served at least once with an overseas command. Air operations were mounted not only against the tribesmen of the North-west Frontier of India, but in Afghanistan, China, Egypt, the Sudan, Somaliland, Iraq, Palestine, Transjordania and Asia Minor. In 1922 the small military forces in Iraq were placed under the command of the Air Officer Commanding-in-Chief, Air Vice-Marshal Sir John Salmond, and the RAF assumed responsibility for the military and air control of the country. Later all other British military forces were withdrawn, and the RAF continued to exercise its responsibilities assisted by the Iraq Army and Assyrian Levies.

Notwithstanding the earlier pronouncement that, against the aeroplane, uncivilised peoples were 'almost helpless', they quickly learned the effectiveness of well-directed rifle fire, as attested by this letter written in 1928 by an RAF officer engaged in the Wahabi War:

'Now for the Shaiba news and the war with ed Dowish. This show is really nasty. He runs a gang of 2,500 well-trained raiders, all very good shots. So far he has shot down three people with direct hits in the radiator. Sqn Ldr Vincent was the first, and he got away with it. Jackson was the next. He was hit in the radiator and came down in the middle of them. Tried to scrap them with his revolver, but was killed —one in the head and the other in the heart. He was found later, stripped, but not mutilated. Next young Kellett was shot down in the same way, but landed over a ridge out of sight. He got away with both locks and bolts out of his guns, and collected all his ammunition before they appeared. . . . Our people dare not fly below 3,000 feet now, as they are shot up at once.

Two Vickers went with four 500-pounders, and nine 9As with Coopers. The photographs were good, and they show that one 500-pounder got a lot of sixty. They bombed the fort with the big stuff and all ran out and met the Coopers outside. . . .'

Such could be the perils, and potential destructiveness, of air control.

From the foregoing it will have been gathered that a standard type of aircraft used for air control was the de Havilland D.H.9A, from the basic design of which a successor, the Westland Wapiti, was developed. These were robust single-engined two-seat biplanes which, as adapted for operations overseas, accumulated a remarkable series of excrescences, such as a spare wheel, desert rations, a water skin or containers for beer bottles, and picketing gear. Jointly with their external armament this gained for them the reputation of carrying 'everything except the kitchen sink'.

It was not, however, in 'policing' operations alone that the RAF can be considered to have exercised air control. One unwarlike, though none the less significant, achievement was the establishment of an air mail service between Cairo and Baghdad—an instance of policemen turned postmen. Furthermore, the 'showing-the-flag' cruises, notably that of 27,000 miles (43,450 km) to Australia and back by Supermarine Southampton flying-boats, served notice that the RAF policemen had long arms. That they offered real protection to British citizens in foreign lands was evident when families were evacuated from Kabul in Vickers Victoria troop-carriers, over 10,000 ft (3,050 m) mountains during one of the most severe winters on record.

Although the D.H.9A and Wapiti merited their official classification as 'general-purpose' aircraft they were essentially bombers, descended from the D.H.4 of 1916. Aircraft even better qualified to share their 'GP' classification were the Italian Caproni monoplanes, developed specially for colonial operations. In being high-wing, strut-braced monoplanes they contrasted sharply with the British biplanes, and a capacious fuselage with enclosed cabin enabled them to serve not only as bombers and reconnaissance aircraft but as transports also. Of these the tri-motor Ca 101 entered service shortly before the Italian campaign against Abyssinia, in the course of which it served not only for attack but in maintaining supplies. Also employed in the same campaign was a similar aircraft having only a single engine and designated Ca 111; later still came the Ca 133, which reverted to the three-engined formula. This last-named type was used to transport Italian paratroops in the invasion of Albania, and its relatively roomy fuselage may have suggested its nicknames of *Caprona* (she-goat) and *Vacca* (cow). These appellations seem somewhat invidious, having regard to the fact that the British biplanes could exhibit quite bovine characteristics (especially when carrying objects underneath) yet have commonly been styled 'workhorses'.

For operations in the French colonies, Breguet single-engined biplanes were generally employed, though experimental examples of a new class known as *type coloniale* were built. One of these, three-engined like the Ca 101 and 133, had the sides of the fuselage entirely cut away, the top then forming a sort of canopy for the rear gunner. Thus protected from colonial suns, he could doubtless have made his contribution to air control with a degree of comfort beyond the dreams of the crews who did the pioneering—with everything except the kitchen sink.

Left: The spare wheel carried by this D.H.9A of No 30 Squadron was typical of the appendages which tended to sprout on air control machines. It was not unusual to see a goatskin of water dangling from the cockpit

Top: The D.H.10, less well-known than most de Havilland designs, was just too late to see action in the first World War. This D.H.10 of 216 Squadron helped to establish the Cairo-Baghdad mail service across the desert in 1921

Above: The Vickers Vincent, with 660 hp Pegasus engine, was the type which finally replaced the Wapiti and Fairey IIIF in 1934. Operated entirely overseas, in the Middle East, Africa and India, the Vincent was in action in Iraq as late as 1941

Centre right: The Hawker Hart two-seat day bomber was one of the family of combat aircraft with which the company's great chief designer, Sydney Camm, made his mark in the 'thirties. When it entered service in 1930, RAF fighter squadrons tried in vain to catch it

Bottom right: Best-remembered RAF floatplane of the air control era was the Fairey IIID, with 450 hp Napier Lion engine

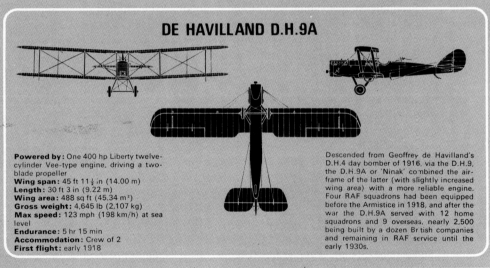

DE HAVILLAND D.H.9A

Powered by: One 400 hp Liberty twelve-cylinder Vee-type engine, driving a two-blade propeller
Wing span: 45 ft 11½ in (14.00 m)
Length: 30 ft 3 in (9.22 m)
Wing area: 488 sq ft (45.34 m²)
Gross weight: 4,645 lb (2,107 kg)
Max speed: 123 mph (198 km/h) at sea level
Endurance: 5 hr 15 min
Accommodation: Crew of 2
First flight: early 1918

Descended from Geoffrey de Havilland's D.H.4 day bomber of 1916, via the D.H.9, the D.H.9A or 'Ninak' combined the airframe of the latter (with slightly increased wing area) with a more reliable engine. Four RAF squadrons had been equipped before the Armistice in 1918, and after the war the D.H.9A served with 12 home squadrons and 9 overseas, nearly 2,500 being built by a dozen British companies and remaining in RAF service until the early 1930s.

CAPRONI Ca 111

Powered by: One 970 hp Isotta-Fraschini Asso 750 RC eighteen-cylinder W-type engine, driving a four-blade propeller
Wing span: 64 ft 6¾ in (19.68 m)
Length: 50 ft 2½ in (15.30 m)
Wing area: 664.13 sq ft (61.70 m²)
Gross weight: 11,795 lb (5,350 kg)
Max speed: 186 mph (300 km/h)
Range: 1,245 miles (2,000 km)
Accommodation: Crew of 3/4

The Ca 111 was typical of the range of 'colonial' aeroplanes of the early 1930s which, in Italy, were almost the exclusive prerogative of the Caproni company. They derived from the Ca 97 and were built to a basic formula allowing them to be powered by one, two or three engines. Although ordered ostensibly for reconnaissance, they carried three or four machine-guns and a small load of bombs, and were used extensively during the Italian campaigns in Africa during the 1930s. Caproni continued the concept later in the decade with a series of twin-engined monoplanes for similar duties, beginning with the Ca 309 Ghibli (Desert Wind) of 1936.

THE GROWTH IN AIRCRAFT ARMAMENT

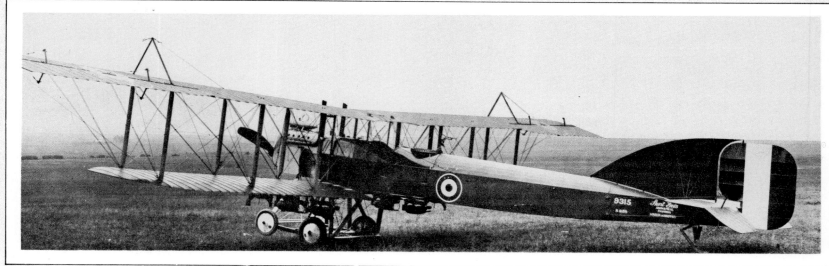

THE FIRST GUN installed on an aeroplane appears to have been a very heavy one, even by modern standards. It was mounted on a Voisin biplane towards the end of 1910 but (mercifully, perhaps, for the crew) was never fired in the air. Nevertheless, a gun of 37-mm calibre was indeed fired from a Voisin before war came in 1914, and guns of this same bore were used fairly extensively by the French in action, mainly in free installations but also rigidly mounted on the Hispano-Suiza engines of Spad fighters, firing through the propeller shaft.

The favoured calibre for aircraft guns was, however, that of the common infantry rifle and machine-gun, and a Springfield '30-06' rifle was apparently the first firearm to be discharged in flight. The date was August 1910; the aircraft a Curtiss pusher biplane. Even before 1914 it was becoming clear that automatic weapons of similar calibre held the greatest promise for aerial use, and the first machine-gun fired in flight (from a Wright biplane in June 1912), was of the newly-invented Lewis drum-fed type. This American weapon was to prove the most successful of its kind used by the Allies in the coming war.

When the war began, no aircraft specifically designed to carry a gun was available to either side. Pistols, carbines, rifles and even shotguns were carried as personal weapons; somewhat later, rifles and Lewis guns were mounted (literally) in lash-up installations. The first truly historic development in air gunnery was the fitting of a fixed machine-gun on one of Anthony Fokker's monoplanes, the firing mechanism being so synchronised with the engine as to allow the gun to fire between the revolving blades of the propeller. The classic type of fixed-gun fighter had thus arrived. Pilot, aeroplane and gun were now, as it were, all of a piece. Aim could be deadly, and deadly indeed was the 'Fokker scourge' of 1915-16.

With the development of synchronising gears in England, the belt-fed Vickers gun was adopted for fixed installations. Like the Fokker's LMG.08—the 'Spandau' beloved of fiction writers—it was based on the Maxim gun. Typical armament for a single-seat fighter as the war approached its end was twin, fixed, rifle-calibre machine-guns, mounted immediately ahead of the pilot so that he could attempt to clear stoppages in flight. Gun-heaters were developed to prevent the lubricating oil from freezing at high altitude, and ammunition belts composed of disintegrating metal links avoided the difficulty of disposing of the earlier continuous canvas belt. The gunsights commonly fitted on Allied fighters were of the elementary ring-and-bead type and the Aldis tubular optical variety. This latter form of sight was not 'telescopic', as is commonly stated.

For free-gun installations many types of mounting were evolved, the most successful being that designed by Warrant Officer Scarff of the RNAS. This took the form of a rotating ring, encircling the gunner and carrying the gun (or sometimes twin guns) on an arm, or bow, capable of elevation or depression.

For many years after the Armistice there were few developments of note in air gunnery. Economy dictated the using-up of war-surplus items, and, although a somewhat improved type of Vickers gun was adopted for the RAF, the standard fighter firepower in that Service remained virtually unchanged from the Sopwith Camel of 1917 to the Gloster Gauntlet of 1934. True, there was the much-publicised Gloster S.S.19 of 1931, with its two Vickers and four Lewis guns; but even this purely experimental installation had been anticipated by the Sopwith Snark of 1918.

Not until the mid-1930s were there any real advances in British fighter armament. During 1937 the first Gloster Gladiators entered service with four Browning guns, of the pattern adopted in succession to the Vickers; but a truly massive increase in firepower came about when no fewer than eight Brownings were specified for the Hurricane and Spitfire. This formidable battery was required by the Air Ministry because it was believed that a pilot would be able to hold his sight (by this time of the illuminated reflector type) 'on target' for a mere two seconds. Only eight Brownings, it was considered, could provide the required 'lethal dose'.

A size of gun favoured during the inter-war years in the USA and Italy was of about ½-inch bore—what the Americans know as a 'fifty caliber'—and it was customary to

Opposite page, top: The Vickers Gunbus of 1915 was claimed to be the first aeroplane designed from the start to carry armament. As no-one had perfected a means of firing between the blades of a turning propeller, it was difficult to mount a front gun on anything but a 'pusher' aircraft of this kind

Centre left: Machine-gun in the rear cockpit of a Blackburn Shark torpedo-spotter-reconnaissance aircraft of the mid-thirties

Centre right: Loading torpedoes on to a squadron of Vickers Vildebeest IVs of the RAF. Two Vildebeest squadrons were used in action against the Japanese invaders of Singapore as late as 1941

Bottom: One of the earliest 'big bombers', this 250 hp Short of the first World War could carry four 230 lb (104 kg) or eight 112 lb (51 kg) bombs and was armed with a single Lewis gun in the rear cockpit

This page, left: The 2,150 lb (975 kg) torpedo carried by the Hawker Horsley was the heaviest weapon of its kind fitted to any landplane when the type entered service in 1928

Below: Fitting a practice torpedo in place between the widely-splayed main undercarriage legs of a Horsley

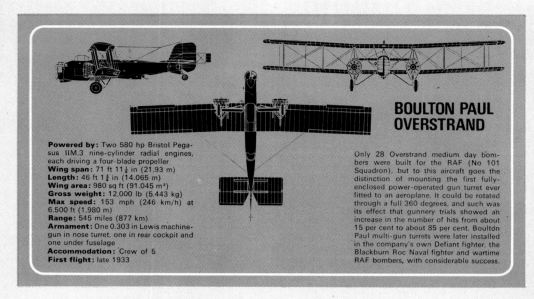

BOULTON PAUL OVERSTRAND

Powered by: Two 580 hp Bristol Pegasus IIM.3 nine-cylinder radial engines, each driving a four-blade propeller
Wing span: 71 ft 11½ in (21.93 m)
Length: 46 ft 1¾ in (14.065 m)
Wing area: 980 sq ft (91.045 m²)
Gross weight: 12,000 lb (5,443 kg)
Max speed: 153 mph (246 km/h) at 6,500 ft (1,980 m)
Range: 545 miles (877 km)
Armament: One 0.303 in Lewis machine-gun in nose turret, one in rear cockpit and one under fuselage
Accommodation: Crew of 5
First flight: late 1933

Only 28 Overstrand medium day bombers were built for the RAF (No 101 Squadron), but to this aircraft goes the distinction of mounting the first fully-enclosed power-operated gun turret ever fitted to an aeroplane. It could be rotated through a full 360 degrees, and such was its effect that gunnery trials showed an increase in the number of hits from about 15 per cent to about 85 per cent. Boulton Paul multi-gun turrets were later installed in the company's own Defiant fighter, the Blackburn Roc Naval fighter and wartime RAF bombers, with considerable success.

mount a gun of this size alongside one of rifle calibre. In France and Germany, however, there was a growing conviction that a more desirable gun would be one of 20-mm calibre, capable of firing explosive ammunition. In the mid-1930s the French tried wing-mounted installations of a new type of 20-mm Hispano-Suiza gun, but found that the wings of fighters of the period were insufficiently stiff to give the desired accuracy of fire. So they continued to favour the engine-mounted installation, or *moteur canon*.

In 1936 a Dewoitine D.510 having such an installation was bought by the British Air Ministry, and later a licence was acquired to build the Hispano-Suiza gun in the United Kingdom. For many years thereafter the 'British-Hispano' was to be the principal weapon of British fighters, though it was not available in quantity for the Battle of Britain. The first British fighter designed specifically for the new gun was, in fact, the Westland Whirlwind; as an interceptor the type was unsuccessful, and the very dense concentration of fire afforded by four 20-mm guns grouped closely in the fuselage nose was employed mainly against ground targets.

When the German Air Force was newly re-created in the early 1930s its first fighters to enter service were biplanes with two rifle-calibre machine-guns; but as thoughts turned to monoplanes, and in particular to the Bf 109, so they turned likewise to 20-mm guns, and a Swiss Oerlikon gun of this calibre was adopted. This was a less hard-hitting gun than the Hispano-Suiza, but was very compact, and fitted well into the wing of the Bf 109. The standard armament of that fighter as used in the Battle of Britain was, in fact, two 20-mm guns in the wing and two of rifle calibre in the fuselage; but the assertion that this armament was 'proved in the Spanish Civil War' is erroneous, for when used in Spain the Bf 109 was armed only with rifle-calibre machine-guns.

One of the most remarkable innovations in the 1930s was the introduction of the power-driven gun turret, enabling the gunner to aim without effort and in comfort. Though the turret in the nose of Britain's Boulton Paul Overstrand bomber is generally hailed as revolutionary in this respect, it must nevertheless be recorded that it was based on French ideas. This was less true of the Frazer-Nash turret installed later on the Hawker Demon two-seater fighter—a forerunner of the 'F-N' turrets familiar on British bombers of the second World War.

The earliest record of bomb-dropping from an aeroplane appears to be the following item in an American newspaper, dated January 1910: 'On Wednesday of last week M Paulhan carried Lt Beck of the US Artillery as passenger on his Henry Farman in order that experiments might be made in the dropping of dummy bombs'. The first live bomb was almost certainly dropped by Lt Myron S Crissy, US Army, in January 1911, and the first bombing raids in warfare were made by the Italians in November of the same year.

Most successful among the bombs developed in the ensuing months was that designed by the Englishman Frederick Marten Hale, who had earlier produced a rifle grenade of a type which was numbered among the heterogeneous collection of weapons pressed into aerial service on the outbreak of war. In British service the Hale's bombs, as they were known, were succeeded by numerous types designed at the Royal Laboratory, and bearing 'RL' designations.

Typical bombs in British service at the war's end were: HERL 250 lb Mk I; HERL 112 lb Mk III; HE Cooper 20 lb; 40 lb Phosphorous Mk I; Baby Incendiary 6½ oz; Thermalloy Incendiary, 34 lb; Bomb, HE 520 lb (Light Case). Generally speaking the HE (high-explosive) bombs were intended for the demolition of such targets as buildings and communications systems and for attacks on submarines, for which there were special adaptations. The Cooper bomb was the outstanding example of the fragmentation type, for use against personnel, and was carried by fighters as well as by bombers. Incendiary bombs, which in some early instances had been filled with petrol, were of several types; and there were special bombs for producing smoke. AP (armour-piercing) and 'SAP' (semi-armour-piercing) bombs were introduced for attacking warships.

One of the earliest practical bomb-sights was developed at the Central Flying School,

as were some of the earliest bomb-carriers; but the best-known sight, which served the RAF in the 1920s and 1930s, was the Wimperis course-setting sight, known in the Service as 'CSBS'. The earliest bombs were dropped by hand, and later by pulling a toggle; but in the 1930s electrical release came into general use. There were numerous types of stowage: if carried externally the bombs were generally horizontal; if internally, either horizontal or suspended vertically by the nose.

The gun and the bomb were quickly joined in the aeronautical armoury by the torpedo, of adapted naval type and bearing no relationship to the 'aerial torpedo' which existed only in popular imagination. The torpedo-dropping aeroplane was developed to its highest pitch in Great Britain. Following pioneering work by Naval officers and the Short and Sopwith companies, the Blackburn company was largely responsible not only for the design and production of suitable aircraft but for developing special methods of carrying, releasing and heating the torpedo, and adjusting it for depth of 'running' in the water. Notwithstanding assertions to the contrary, however, the Italians were the true pioneers of torpedo-dropping. General A Guidoni, one of the greatest names in Italian aeronautics, left record:

'I was ordered in 1912 to help Mr Pateras Pescara, who had suggested to the navy the building of a torpedo-plane. Mr Pescara was a lawyer. Had he been a technical man he would probably have been refused permission to try out his scheme. . . . With my faithful Farman I succeeded in dropping 170 lb (77 kg), so I concluded that with a machine of 6,000 lb (2,720 kg) total weight it would be possible to drop a small torpedo.' Having described the special seaplane he then built the general said: 'With this machine in February 1914 I succeeded in dropping a torpedo of 750 lb (340 kg).'

From that moment, it should have been clear that the aeroplane would one day pose a serious threat to sea power.

Opposite page, top: First RAF bomber to have a power-operated gun turret was the Boulton Paul Overstrand

Bottom: The four-gun Nash and Thompson turret in the tail of the Armstrong Whitworth Whitley bomber. The guns were staggered to facilitate 'feeding' with the belts of ammunition

This page, left: Sir Kingsley Wood, Secretary of State for Air in 1939, tries his hand at firing the Vickers 'K' gun used by air observers. Rate of fire was 1,000-1,100 rounds a minute

Centre: A 2,000 lb (907 kg) bomb waiting to be stowed on board a Whitley of RAF Bomber Command in 1941

Bottom: First squadron to be equipped with Hawker Hurricanes in 1937, and hence the first to fly a modern eight-gun monoplane fighter, was No 111 of RAF Fighter Command

Poland, the Phoney War and the Battle of France

AT 04.30 HOURS on 1 September 1939 three Junkers Ju 87 dive-bombers from Germany's Stukageschwader 1 made an attack on Polish units around the bridge over the Vistula at Tczew; the second World War had begun.

The Poles had a total of just over 300 combat aircraft, comprising roughly equal numbers of fighters and bombers. Most of these, particularly the open-cockpit PZL machines which equipped the fighter units, were between three and seven years old and frankly obsolescent. Bad decisions at the highest level had left the Polish Air Force chronically weak in reserves, and had further dissipated the available forces by splitting them into 'penny packets' around the country, allocating fighter and bomber squadrons in ones and twos to the five Polish land armies. Only the Pursuit Brigade, based around Warsaw for defence of the capital, was in any condition to offer effective resistance; its five squadrons mustered some 50 machines, and were supported by an efficient warning and control system. The other units were spread so thinly that they could never enjoy even local superiority; when liaison and ground facilities broke down under the hammer blows of the Wehrmacht, these isolated groups could only make shift as best they could, and die—superbly.

The units of Kesselring's Luftflotte 1 and Löhr's Luftflotte 4 mustered an effective total of some 1,300 fighting aircraft, comprising 900 bombers and dive-bombers, 200 fighters committed to the offensive, and a further 200 fighters positioned to defend Germany against retaliation. The German estimates of Polish strength erred wildly, and the Luftwaffe was convinced it faced about 900 defending machines. Herein lay the seeds of the old myth that the Polish Air Force was bombed out of existence on the ground. Mobilisation sent the squadrons of the Lotnictwo Wojskowe from their peacetime bases to small combat airstrips which had largely eluded German reconnaissance. When the bases marked on their maps (and the carefully deployed dummy aircraft) had been left in cratered chaos, and when the Germans encountered only

some 150 fighters in the air, they assumed that the rest of those '900 aircraft' had been bombed to scrap. In fact the PZLs were almost exclusively destroyed in aerial combat between 1 and 16 September.

The bomber attacks on Polish airfields, factories, communications and troop concentrations which began on 1 September and continued—when the weather permitted—almost without cease for three weeks met with determined, but necessarily scattered, resistance. The thinly-spread Army Air Forces were hamstrung from the start, and made a really significant contribution only through their bombing attacks on advancing German troops; but the Pursuit Brigade showed by its success on 1 September what a Polish Air Force might have achieved if properly equipped and organised. Two major raids on Warsaw were turned back on that day; in the morning raid not a single bomb fell on the capital, in the afternoon only isolated flights penetrated the defences. Twelve raiding bombers were shot down (four others were destroyed by an Army Air Force squadron in the vicinity) for the loss of 10 PZLs destroyed and 24 damaged.

This success was not, sadly, to become the pattern for Polish defensive operations. The Army Air Forces were unable to offer serious resistance, although the courage with which the handfuls of fighters and bombers rose to contest the skies and to press home low-level raids on armoured columns was nothing less than suicidal. In individual spirit and determination the excellently-trained Polish aircrews were second to none in the world; but more than courage was needed when a thousand enemy aircraft invaded airspace defended by 150. Reduced to threes and fours, exhausted, without fuel, without ground handling and repair facilities, without replacements, bedevilled by conflicting orders, the squadrons bitterly conceded mile after mile.

By 16 September the 50 or so surviving Polish fighters were gathered near Lublin, and about 30 bombers were operating from fields in Volhynia. There was not enough fuel to get even a third of them into the air. The next day, in a long-planned move, Soviet Russia invaded eastern Poland and put paid to any last hope of establishing a defensive line. The surviving combat aircraft were flown into exile in Hungary and Romania by their crews, who now began a long and eventually doomed search for a way to save Poland by sacrificing themselves for the safety of foreign allies. The skies belonged to the Luftwaffe, and the ruthless use it made of that freedom should have warned the world that total war had begun in earnest.

The crucifixion of Poland had cost the Luftwaffe some 280 machines destroyed and a roughly similar number so badly damaged that they were eventually written off. The personnel casualties included 413 trained aircrew killed or missing. These losses lent weight to the orders which held the western front in stasis; to build up the strength of the squadrons would take time, and Luftwaffe units in the west were forbidden to seek combat. There were lessons to be digested; in particular, the effectiveness of obsolescent fighters, when flown with determination, had been greater than anticipated.

In the west the picture was one of hesitancy and indecision. Statesmen who had not yet faced the reality of war still hoped for a political settlement, and felt that their military obligations were fulfilled by maintaining a relatively peaceful status quo throughout the winter of 1939-40. German air activity over Britain was confined to isolated attacks of no real significance, on ports and shipping, and flights by single Dornier reconnaissance machines which played hide-and-seek with the RAF in the winter clouds. Two RAF formations— the Advanced Air Striking Force of Blenheim and Battle light bombers supported by Nos 1 and 73 Hurricane Squadrons, and Nos 85 and 87 Hurricane Squadrons supporting the Air Component in the extreme north-east of France—had been sent to the continent in September. French appeals for a larger contribution led to the despatch of two Gladiator squadrons to the Air Component in November. Air Marshal Dowding, commanding RAF Fighter Command, was even at this stage unwilling to weaken his Home Defence network by stripping it of any further Hurricanes.

The Allied fighter strength in France and the Low Countries in the spring of 1940 totalled perhaps 550 French types (of which the majority were obsolescent Morane-Saulnier MS.406 monoplanes, and only 36 were Dewoitine D.520s); some 40 Hurricanes and 20 Gladiators; and a few score Dutch and Belgian machines, of which not more than two dozen were of a quality even faintly comparable to current German equipment. When Hitler had secured his northern flank by occupying Norway and Denmark in April—a campaign involving a heroic but hopeless defence by pitifully weak Norwegian and RAF forces—he was free to concentrate on blitzkrieg in the west; and on 10 May 1940 the war stopped being a 'phoney' with shocking suddenness. The story is too well documented to repeat in detail here: the heavy and co-ordinated attacks on airfields, rail centres, aircraft factories and road bottlenecks; the constant

strafing attacks by single- and twin-engined fighters; the surgical removal of strong-points and blocking positions by dive-bombers; the humiliating and exhausting retreat of the Allied squadrons from airfield to airfield, until only the sea lay behind them. In pure aviation terms there was no secret, no lesson to be learned—except that 1,000 modern fighters can beat 600 obsolescent ones.

The real lesson of German success in 1939 and the spring of 1940 was, in fact, that 'pure aviation' was secondary to the intelligent co-ordination of all arms—land, sea and air. Blitzkrieg was no magical formula by which defeat could be turned into victory, no secret technique by which the weaker could defeat the stronger. To succeed it required forces of comparable if not superior strength, and definitely superior equipment. It required an impetus to be built up through the elements of surprise, and maintained by tireless advance; its cumulative effect was everything, while each of its separate elements could have been defeated by the forces which opposed it, if dealt with in isolation. Long-range raids by medium bombers could be turned back or broken up; they were turned back at Warsaw, and they were later to be broken up over Kent.

Dive-bombers could not survive in skies defended by modern, co-ordinated fighter forces, well controlled and forewarned. Paratroop landings were necessarily of limited strength and lightly equipped, and could be isolated and engulfed by cool defenders before they could do serious

harm—as in the early days of the battle for Crete. Strafing sweeps were harder to counter, but by themselves could not turn a determined defence into a rout. Yet the combination of all these types of operation, backed by strong ground forces advancing on unexpected axes and accompanied by their own mobile anti-aircraft batteries, proved overwhelming.

The defenders lacked a unifying command, a contingency plan, stable ground facilities and proven early warning networks; most of all they lacked the hardware. The attacker had been bending every sinew, for years on end, to build up large and well-trained forces equipped with the most modern equipment, and to shape those forces according to sound tactical principles. The defender had allowed his technology to starve and his tactical thinking to stagnate. Sheer technical brilliance is nothing unless the political will exists to back it, buy it, and consider how it may best be employed. It has been one of the great tragedies of our time that this will seems to grow lustily in the soil of dictatorships, and to wither and die in democracies.

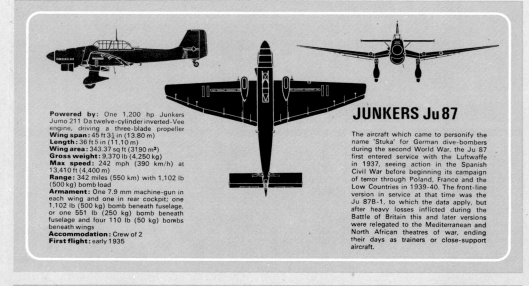

JUNKERS Ju 87

Powered by: One 1,200 hp Junkers Jumo 211 Da twelve-cylinder inverted-Vee engine, driving a three-blade propeller
Wing span: 45 ft 3¼ in (13.80 m)
Length: 36 ft 5 in (11.10 m)
Wing area: 343.37 sq ft (3190 m²)
Gross weight: 9,370 lb (4,250 kg)
Max speed: 242 mph (390 km/h) at 13,410 ft (4,400 m)
Range: 342 miles (550 km) with 1,102 lb (500 kg) bomb load
Armament: One 7.9 mm machine-gun in each wing and one in rear cockpit; one 1,102 lb (500 kg) bomb beneath fuselage, or one 551 lb (250 kg) bomb beneath fuselage and four 110 lb (50 kg) bombs beneath wings
Accommodation: Crew of 2
First flight: early 1935

The aircraft which came to personify the name 'Stuka' for German dive-bombers during the second World War, the Ju 87 first entered service with the Luftwaffe in 1937, seeing action in the Spanish Civil War before beginning its campaign of terror through Poland, France and the Low Countries in 1939-40. The front-line version in service at that time was the Ju 87B-1, to which the data apply, but after heavy losses inflicted during the Battle of Britain this and later versions were relegated to the Mediterranean and North African theatres of war, ending their days as trainers or close-support aircraft.

MORANE-SAULNIER MS.406

Powered by: One 860 hp Hispano-Suiza 12Y 31 twelve-cylinder Vee-type engine, driving a 9 ft 10 in (3.00 m) diameter three-blade propeller
Wing span: 34 ft 9¾ in (10.61 m)
Length: 26 ft 9¼ in (8.17 m)
Wing area: 172.22 sq ft (16.00 m²)
Gross weight: 5,600 lb (2,540 kg)
Max speed: 304 mph (490 km/h) at 14,750 ft (4,500 m)
Range: 685 miles (1,100 km)
Armament: One 20 mm Hispano-Suiza cannon firing through propeller hub and one 7.5 mm machine-gun in each wing
Accommodation: Crew of 1
First flight: (MS.405 prototype): 8 August 1935
Upon the outbreak of the second World War the MS.406 stood in the same relation to the Armée de l'Air as did the Hurricane to the RAF—that of being, numerically, its most important fighter available to meet the German onslaught. Some 300 of these French fighters were then in service in France, and more than 1,000 were eventually built; but, gallantly though they

were flown, their technical inferiority to the Luftwaffe's fighters and their own shortcomings—poor finish, inadequate armament and inefficient engines, among others—enabled them to produce only a fraction of the opposition that their numbers warranted.

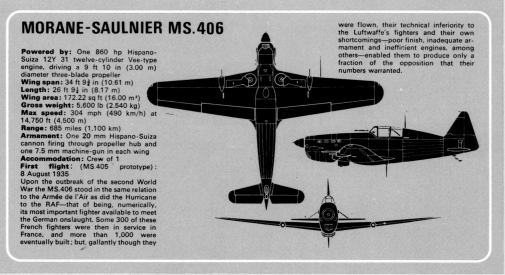

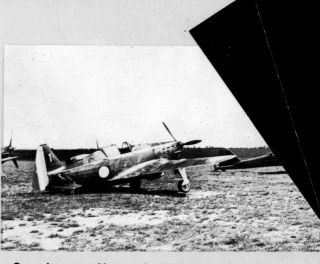

Opposite page: Airmen of a Battle day-bomber unit of the RAF's Advanced Air Striking Force warm themselves by a fire in a truly Artic setting in France during the winter of the 'Phoney' war

This page, top left: The DC-2s and DC-3s of KLM proclaimed their nationality, and optimistic neutrality, in no uncertain manner in the autumn of 1939

Left: The Fairey Battles of the AASF were to pay dearly for their attempts to stem the German advance in May-June 1940. Excellent when first flown, they were outdated and almost defenceless by the outbreak of war

Above: A Morane-Saulnier MS.406 of one of the French squadrons that flew side-by-side with the AASF. Since nationalisation in the mid-thirties, the French aircraft industry had produced but a trickle of modern combat aircraft, though several fine designs had reached the prototype and pre-series stages

Below: By far the best of the French fighters in service in 1940 was the Dewoitine D.520, of which this example survives in the Musée de l'Air in Paris. Only 36 were operational at the time of the German blitzkrieg

RADAR

Above: A modern secondary radar display at London Airport. The early types of warning radar used during the second World War were often 'cluttered' with many extraneous signals

Right: A Wellington XIII of RAF Coastal Command, festooned with the aerials of wartime ASV (air-to-surface vessel) radar

Above: The first radar for night fighters to go into large-scale service was the British AI (Airborne Interception) Mark IV, seen here fitted to a Beaufighter VI. The arrow-shaped aerial on the nose belonged to the transmitter. The pairs of aerials on the wings belonged to the receiver; when the signals picked up by each of the wing aerials were equal in strength, the target was dead ahead. Range was about $3\frac{1}{2}$ miles (5.5 km) at 18,000 ft (5,500 m)

Left: By 1941 it was possible to pack airborne radar into a 'thimble' nose installation as shown on this YP-61 Black Widow night fighter

Opposite page, top: First radar to be used operationally was the British Chain Home system. The transmitter aerials were suspended between the three 350-ft (107-m) high towers to the left of the picture. The receiver aerials were suspended between the four 240-ft (73-m) towers on the right. Maximum range was about 110 miles (177 km)

Centre: Head of the British research team which perfected radar pre-war was Sir Robert Watson Watt (centre)

Bottom left: Aerials of the German Lichtenstein radar, on the nose of a Junkers Ju 88 night fighter

Bottom right: Electronic countermeasures have always gone hand-in-hand with radar. This picture of the RAF's wartime Operation Corona in action shows the 'ghost voice' microphone over which false messages were passed to enemy night fighters, as if from German radar controllers. Also visible are receivers tuned to German transmissions and a gramophone for jumbled-voice jamming

NOWADAYS RADAR PLAYS a vitally important role in every aspect of air warfare. Using it, fighters are able to hunt down their prey by day or night in all but the very worst weather. Bombers are able to investigate precisely, and aim their deadly loads at targets unseen by their crews. Maritime aircraft are able to detect submarines which expose any part of their structure above the surface of the sea. The list of applications of radar in modern warfare is almost endless.

It was not always so. Prior to 1936 the only means of locating aircraft beyond visual range was with the sound locator. This massive device had a maximum range of about eight miles (13 km) if all went well—but it rarely did. Even against the old biplane bombers this was barely adequate, for eight miles meant a warning time of only about four minutes. The 1930s saw a revolution in aircraft design, during which the speeds of bombers

doubled. Clearly, the defenders needed something much better than the sound locator if they were to get their fighters into position in time to intercept the raiding bombers.

The answer was radar, a device which beamed out high-powered pulses of radio energy and received, amplified and displayed the feeble echo signals bounced back from any aircraft in the path of the beam. Even in 1936 such ideas were not new: as early as 1904 a German inventor named Christian Hülsmeyer had patented a design for a crude radar set. But it was not until the 1930s that the science of electronics had progressed sufficiently for a radar to be built which was able to detect aircraft at ranges beyond those possible with sound locators.

Once the know-how necessary for radar existed, development was rapid. In June 1936 the first experimental radar built by a British research team under Robert Watson Watt was able to detect an aircraft flying 17 miles (27 km) away. The following month an improved set detected an

aircraft at 40 miles (65 km). By the end of September ranges in excess of 55 miles (88 km) were commonplace.

As the war clouds gathered over Europe, men of the Royal Air Force struggled to erect a chain of twenty early-warning radar ground stations along the east coast of Britain. When war broke out in September 1939 the initial chain was complete, and able to detect aircraft flying at 15,000 ft (4,570 m) approaching from the east or south almost anywhere between the northern tip of Scotland and Portsmouth; by this time the radars used had a maximum range of about 110 miles (177 km). When the real test came, during the Battle of Britain in the summer of 1940, these so-called Chain Home radars proved their value time and time again, by providing information which enabled the hard-pressed squadrons of RAF Fighter Command to be used to maximum effect.

The Chain Home radar was a very large piece of equipment: the installation weighed several tons, with three 350-ft (107 m) high towers to carry the trans-

mitter aerials and four 240-ft (73 m) high towers to carry the separate receiver aerials. With this in mind it was, therefore, with some trepidation that Dr Edward Bowen and his team had begun work before the war on a radar set small enough to fit into an aircraft. But it was done, and late in 1937 the first crude airborne radar, occupying most of the cabin of a twin-engined Anson, was able to detect ships out to ranges of about 10 miles (16 km). A refinement of this device, able to detect other aircraft and code-named AI (for Airborne Interception), entered service in Fighter Command in the summer of 1940. During the early morning darkness of 23 July 1940, Flying Officer G Ashfield and his radar operator, Sergeant R Leyland, in a Blenheim fighter, made history when they used AI radar for the first time to assist in shooting down an enemy bomber.

As the war expanded, so did the uses of radar. Coastal Command aircraft operating far out over the Atlantic carried ASV (Air-to-Surface-Vessel) radar to hunt down submarines running on the surface; during the Battle of the Atlantic aircraft sank more than 250 submarines, and assisted surface vessels to destroy more than 40 others. In the early hours of 8 June 1944, Flying Officer K Moore and his crew, flying an ASV-equipped Liberator, made skilful use of radar when they destroyed two German submarines in a space of only twenty minutes.

RAF Bomber Command made use of the Gee device to navigate to and from targets, while aircraft of the Pathfinder Force carried the precision-bombing Oboe and H2S radars to enable them to mark out the targets for the main-force bombers following behind. When the American daylight bombing offensive got under way, the bombers carried a radar similar to H2S, so that attacks could be made through overcast.

During the large-scale paratroop assault which preceded the invasion of Normandy in June 1944, it was the low-powered Eureka radar beacons which marked out the dropping zones for the many hundreds of transport aircraft.

The development of radar in Germany began, quite independently, at about the same time as that in Britain. Initially the rate of development was much slower. However, the Allied bomber attacks on the German homeland forced the Luftwaffe to devote considerable effort to building up its own chain of defensive radar stations in occupied Europe and Germany itself, and for the German night fighters there was a lightweight airborne radar, code-named Lichtenstein. The battle between the German defences and the British night bombers reached its climax during the night of 30 March 1944, when the defenders shot down 94 out of a total of 795 bombers attacking Nuremburg; the great majority fell to radar-equipped night fighters.

During the years between 1936 and 1945, in the forcing-house of war, threatened or actual, radar blossomed from a dream in a scientist's mind into a vast family of devices which revolutionised air warfare. Since the end of the war, development work has continued without pause, for today victory in air combat will go—other things being equal—to the man flying the aircraft with the best radar and weapons system, rather than the man flying the machine with the best performance.

Bottom left: The cupola under the rear fuselage of this Lancaster bomber housed the rotating scanner of the H2S ground mapping radar. The 'H' shaped aerial immediately behind the nose gun turret belonged to the Rebecca device; used in conjunction with a Eureka ground beacon, this enabled the crew to home on their base airfield from more than 60 miles (96 km) away

Above, top to bottom:
By the end of the second World War radar sets were becoming very small indeed. The transmitter and aerial system of the AN/APS 6 radar fitted to these Grumman F6F Hellcat night fighters was so small and light that it could be mounted far along the starboard wing without creating problems due to its asymmetric position

Lichtenstein SN2 radar aerials on the nose of a Messerschmitt Bf 110G-4/R7 night fighter

The aerial of the AI Mark VIII radar was only 5 cm long; it was mounted at the focus of a reflector disc and could be aimed at objects in the same way as a spotlight. It could locate targets with much greater precision than the earlier AI Mark IV; maximum range was $4\frac{1}{2}$ miles (7.25 km) even if the night fighter was only 5,000 ft (1,525 m) above the ground. The aircraft is a Beaufighter, with nose fairing removed

The USAAF's tandem-cockpit radar-equipped P-38 Night Lightning of 1944 could be used both to search for enemy night bombers and as a nocturnal prowler armed with guns, rockets and bombs

Battle of Britain

NAMED WITH HIS PRACTISED eye for the dramatic by Prime Minister Winston Churchill, who took office on 10 May 1940 as the war leader against Germany, the Battle of Britain was the inevitable outcome of confrontation with Europe's aggressor. Ever since the Kaiser's war, in which a mild foretaste of air attack against British civil life had been administered, the Royal Air Force had been husbanding and deploying its strength against a repetition of such an assault—at first from France and later, in the 'thirties, from Germany herself. Despite the clouded intentions of Hitler's real ambitions, the British air defences grew rapidly during the last months of peace; yet not even the most sanguine prophet could foretell the magnitude of disaster that would bring the loss of France and the Low Countries in May and June 1940. Within those two months the most powerful air force in the world arrived on the northern coast of Europe, flushed with scarcely-disputed victory over a half-dozen nations.

Against almost 3,000 Junkers, Heinkels, Dorniers and Messerschmitts, deployed from Norway to the coast of Spain, Britain's Fighter Command mustered at the beginning of July barely 50 squadrons of Hurricanes, Spitfires, Blenheims and Defiants, many of which had suffered crippling losses

in the retreat from France and in the skies over Dunkirk. Nevertheless the structures of defence had been well founded; the nation had nurtured a prolific aircraft industry in the years of peace and now the flow of new fighters did not falter. Fighter Command's chief, Air Marshal Dowding, had been the brilliant architect of a scientific defence—close-knit, with well-deployed airfields interlaced with tight systems of raid reporting and control of fighters. Most vital of these systems was the radar chain, far advanced beyond any in the world, and already an integrated link that permitted economy of effort by the weakened fighter squadrons.

Reichsmarschall Hermann Göring paused only briefly before launching his attack on Britain with Luftflotten (Air Fleets) 2 and 3 from France and the Low Countries. His attacks were mounted as a means of drawing Fighter Command into the air where, as an opening gambit to the invasion of Britain, it would be destroyed as surely as had been the air forces of Poland, Norway, Holland, Belgium and France.

July wore on as the German attacks increased in weight, with numerous raids mounted against convoys sailing in the English Channel and along the east coast. While the German High Command finalised

Top: No picture could symbolise better the preparation within Fighter Command for the inevitable battle to come than this line-up of new Mk I Spitfires

Centre: Partner of the Spitfire in the summer of 1940 was Sydney Camm's Hurricane. The lower aircraft bears a chequerboard badge signifying that its pilot was Polish

Bottom: Three Junkers Ju 88 day bombers of the Luftwaffe. Experience in the Battle of Britain led to later versions having more powerful engines, more armour protection, heavier defensive armament and a bigger bomb-load

Above left: A Spitfire pilot warms up his Merlin engine for take-off

Left: Although outnumbered by Hurricanes the Battle of Britain Spitfires caught the imagination of the public, as even the least technically-minded housewife could recognise easily their 'pointed' wings

Top: The Operations Room at Fighter Command HQ, Bentley Priory, in 1940. The officers on the dais look down on WAAF plotters who display the progress of raids and interceptions with symbols on a map table

Above: Wearing their 'Mae West' lifejackets, pilots of a Spitfire squadron wait tensely for the next call to 'scramble'

Below: Enthusiasts will argue forever the relative merits of the Hurricane and Spitfire. In fact, without either type the Battle of Britain would have been lost

plans for the coming invasion and Hitler called on Britain to surrender, the stabbing attacks against shipping attained their aim —the sapping of defence energy and the grinding of nerves through enforced patrols. Little damage was done among the merchant vessels, but the attrition suffered by Dowding's pilots threatened disaster even before the main attack was met.

The attacks on coastal shipping were accompanied by air raids on the ports and naval bases of Portland, Portsmouth and Dover. This enabled the Luftwaffe to achieve one of its first objectives during July, for its depredations forced the Admiralty to withdraw most British naval forces from the Channel to bases further afield, with the result that scarcely a single convoy could pass through the Dover Straits during the first week in August. Nevertheless, this in turn deprived the Luftwaffe of its favoured targets and thereby gave respite to the weary pilots of No. 11 Group who were defending the all-important south-east under the energetic leadership of Air Marshal Keith Park.

No-one in Britain during that lull dared believe other than that Göring was flexing his muscles for the great attack. And so it transpired. From 8 August the avalanche gained momentum. Enemy formations which had hitherto comprised little more than a Staffel of bombers (about eight aircraft) now appeared as a mass of 50 or more with a like number of escorting fighters. At first it seemed that the British

must be overwhelmed; but as Dowding's commanders recognised the German strength, more fighters were scrambled and successively fed into the fight. Radar gave these commanders eyes in the sky and by their tactics the enemy's determination was eroded as raid after raid was turned back.

Already strengths and weaknesses were being exploited. The much-vaunted Junkers Ju 87—the screaming personification of the 'Stuka' dive-bomber—was seen to be easy prey to Spitfires and Hurricanes, for in its dive it was a steady target while its escort was powerless to save it. Diving Stukas fell with flaming trails to litter the summer fields of southern England. Göring's favourite fighter, the Messerschmitt Bf 110 Zerstörer (destroyer) was cumbersome as a bomber escort and losses among Zerstörergeschwadern soon forced the Germans to provide escorts for the escort!

Climax of the planned German air assault (Adlerangriff) was scheduled for 13 August, but bad weather brought delay until Thursday the 15th. On that day Göring launched his 'eagles' from all flanks of his command, from Luftflotte 5 in Norway and Denmark, and from Luftflotten 2 and 3 in Holland, Belgium and France. From mid-morning until late evening the great raids came and went, huge armadas of fighters and bombers feinting and striking, probing and thrusting, carpeting the British airfields with bombs and bullets. But try though they might they found scarcely a flaw in the air defences. Pilots of the British fighters flew and flew again, sweating and straining, turning and

weaving their white patterns against the blue sky. Many fell, others struggled home on tattered wings to find a fresh fighter. From Yorkshire to Dorset was heard the crash of bomb, the rattle of gunfire high above.

The battle died with the sun that day. Almost every enemy tactic failed and Fighter Command held firm. This had been Dowding's sternest test. For the loss of 28 fighters destroyed and 13 damaged, from which all but 12 pilots escaped, the Royal Air Force and anti-aircraft guns destroyed 75 enemy aircraft. More significant, the Luftwaffe, through extraordinarily inept intelligence, failed to destroy a single airfield vital to the defence. Furthermore, so roughly treated were the formations flying from Scandinavia that Göring never again launched Luftflotte 5 in any concerted strength against Britain.

Scarcely daunted by its losses elsewhere on this 'Black Thursday', the Luftwaffe was now committed to all-out attack, believing as it did that crippling losses had been inflicted on Dowding's fighters. The Germans returned day after day throughout the remainder of August. By skilful 'rotation' of squadrons to and from the relative quiet of the north, Dowding strove to bolster his defences round London and the south-east.

But the strain began to show. The battle-trained ranks of squadron and section leaders thinned from combat strain and casualties. Young men became veterans at nineteen. Ground-crews dropped from the sheer fatigue of sleepless nights spent repair-

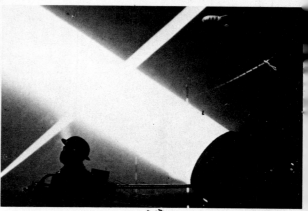

ing the damaged fighters. Yet this was the glorious time of Churchill's 'Few'; great names like Stanford Tuck, Douglas Bader, 'Ginger' Lacey, Brian Kingcome, Peter Townsend, Don Kingaby, Johnnie Kent, Colin Gray, 'Sailor' Malan and 'Sawn-off' Lock were engraved bright on the tablets of British history to reflect the drama of those heroic days. Men had come from many countries to fly among the ranks of Fighter Command; indeed, it was a Czech, Josef Frantisek, who topped the Allied score of enemy aircraft destroyed before he met his death after one month in action.

As Fighter Command's ordeal approached its climax of terrible exhaustion, there emerged within the echelons of Göring's airmen, too, all the signs of strain, frustration and discouragement, of demoralisation and disenchantment—all the signs of spent determination. For two months the German crews had fought with elan and courage, had met the shock of successive combats, had seen their friends fall in blazing bombers and—too often—simply lost comrades without trace or knowledge of their fate. The fighter pilots, seldom able to penetrate far over the British mainland or divest themselves of their responsibilities of escort to the bombers, fought the constant threat of fuel shortage, often falling not to the guns of British fighters but to the grey waves of a hostile Channel.

This frustration permeated to the fractious Reichsmarschall who, breaking all the rules of war and perpetrating one of

history's classic blunders, suddenly shifted the aim of his attack on 7 September. While Dowding's pilots waited all day for the coming attack, Göring himself arrived on the Channel coast to watch his great armadas pass. Not the British airfields, nor the coastal towns in daylight . . but London at dusk and in darkness. This was to be his point of aim: to break the spirit of the Briton at home. To smash his capital, to lay waste his homes. To destroy his will to make war.

That night a new era of warfare was born, with the ravages of Junkers, Heinkel and the rest. Hundreds of black-crossed bombers droned their way along the Thames to London. Time and again the great shoals of Dorniers shuddered as swift stabs by Spitfires pierced the hostile ranks. But as darkness fell the bombs crashed down, on the sprawling dockland of London, on the close-packed homes of the poor, on the food stores of Britain's capital: on the greatest target on earth.

This was London's ordeal by fire. In streets aflame with incendiary, in blasted brick and cruel shards of driven glass, the ordinary man and woman faced the terror of the new air age, the terror that had come a little earlier to Warsaw and Rotterdam. This was to be the new ordeal—the raid that would last for fifty nights.

Yet it was this raid, in all its horror, that was to spell salvation to the island race; for in that moment of deflected aim Dowding's men gained strength anew, and when, with one final fling, the Luftwaffe turned

again on Britain by day on 15 September, the Hurricanes and Spitfires—which had been too often 'destroyed' in German propaganda—dealt so severely with the raiders that the attack faltered and broke, never again to return in like strength by day.

True, the battle waxed and waned for six more weeks, but the attack had failed. Hitler abandoned his plans for invasion of the British islands, for winter was upon him. Henceforth his gaze turned towards the East. Had he but known, the shift of Göring's aim against British cities had sown the seeds of an ill wind. In time the German nation would reap the whirlwind of great raids by bombers based in the islands it had failed to conquer from the skies of that fateful summer.

At the time, with all the uncertainties of war unresolved, victory and defeat in the Battle of Britain represented not so much the blunting of the Nazi weapon of aggression as the survival of the British will to stand and defend the free world. The fact that Göring's Luftwaffe also survived as a force in being must blur the traditional concept of clear-cut victor and vanquished. Yet not even the passage of years has dimmed the feat of arms gained by those few men of the RAF. No academic analysis by theorists can ever cloud the fact that between that September and Armageddon stood and flew and fought just 3,080 men —the equivalent of an infantry brigade or a warship's crew—and the world lived to fight another day.

Opposite page, top: The harvest fields of southern England bore a strange crop in the summer of 1940. This Bf 109 was crash-landed by its wounded pilot in a cornfield at Berwick, near Eastbourne. When captured he commented: 'That's what we get for coming to England'

Upper left: Before—a Heinkel He 111H-6 waiting to take off

Lower left: After—the remains of an He 111 dominate one of the many graveyards of the Luftwaffe created by the air battles of the second World War

Centre, top to bottom:
When this Bf 110 crash-landed on the south-east coast, other German aircraft tried to destroy it with their bombs. They missed by 20 yards (18 m)

Wolf in sheep's clothing: this Bf 109E was captured intact and test flown by RAF pilots to learn its capabilities and weaknesses

Driven from the daylight skies, the Luftwaffe was forced to seek the cover of darkness for its raids from September 1940. So began the grim testing time of the 'night blitz' for the people of London

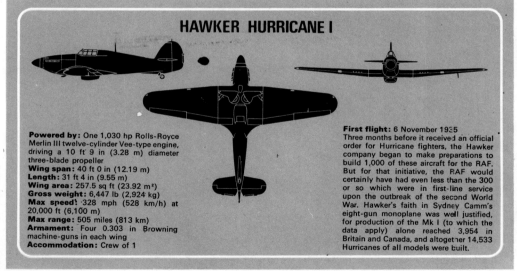

HAWKER HURRICANE I

Powered by: One 1,030 hp Rolls-Royce Merlin III twelve-cylinder Vee-type engine, driving a 10 ft 9 in (3.28 m) diameter three-blade propeller
Wing span: 40 ft 0 in (12.19 m)
Length: 31 ft 4 in (9.55 m)
Wing area: 257.5 sq ft (23.92 m²)
Gross weight: 6,447 lb (2,924 kg)
Max speed: 328 mph (528 km/h) at 20,000 ft (6,100 m)
Max range: 505 miles (813 km)
Armament: Four 0.303 in Browning machine-guns in each wing
Accommodation: Crew of 1

First flight: 6 November 1935
Three months before it received an official order for Hurricane fighters, the Hawker company began to make preparations to build 1,000 of these aircraft for the RAF. But for that initiative, the RAF would certainly have had even less than the 300 or so which were in first-line service upon the outbreak of the second World War. Hawker's faith in Sydney Camm's eight-gun monoplane was well justified, for production of the Mk I (to which the data apply) alone reached 3,954 in Britain and Canada, and altogether 14,533 Hurricanes of all models were built.

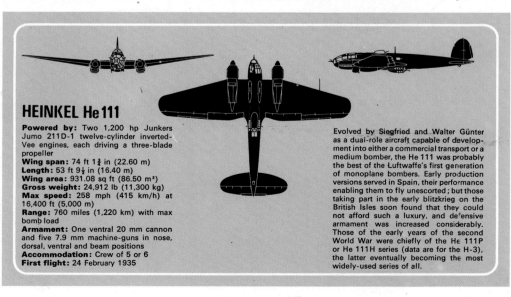

HEINKEL He 111

Powered by: Two 1,200 hp Junkers Jumo 211D-1 twelve-cylinder inverted-Vee engines, each driving a three-blade propeller
Wing span: 74 ft 1¾ in (22.60 m)
Length: 53 ft 9½ in (16.40 m)
Wing area: 931.08 sq ft (86.50 m²)
Gross weight: 24,912 lb (11,300 kg)
Max speed: 258 mph (415 km/h) at 16,400 ft (5,000 m)
Range: 760 miles (1,220 km) with max bomb load
Armament: One ventral 20 mm cannon and five 7.9 mm machine-guns in nose, dorsal, ventral and beam positions
Accommodation: Crew of 5 or 6
First flight: 24 February 1935

Evolved by Siegfried and Walter Günter as a dual-role aircraft capable of development into either a commercial transport or a medium bomber, the He 111 was probably the best of the Luftwaffe's first generation of monoplane bombers. Early production versions served in Spain, their performance enabling them to fly unescorted; but those taking part in the early blitzkrieg on the British Isles soon found that they could not afford such a luxury, and defensive armament was increased considerably. Those of the early years of the second World War were chiefly of the He 111P or He 111H series (data are for the H-3), the latter eventually becoming the most widely-used series of all.

This page, top left: After early operations had revealed serious deficiencies in their defensive armament, the Handley Page Hampdens of Bomber Command were fitted with twin Vickers guns in their dorsal and ventral positions, armour plate and flame-damping exhausts. After that they took part successfully in many night raids, including the first attack on Berlin and the thousand-bomber raid on Cologne

Top right: Sgt John Hannah, a wireless operator/air gunner of No 83 Squadron, was awarded the Victoria Cross for putting out fires that would have destroyed his Hampden on the night of 15/16 September 1940. The aircraft was hit over Antwerp while engaged in an attack on German barges assembled for the invasion of England

Centre: The industry that made the RAF bomber offensive possible is typified by this photograph of girl workers with Merlin engines, used in aircraft such as the Lancaster and Mosquito

Opposite page, top left: Wartime Lancaster sorties totalled about 156,000, during which 608,612 tons of bombs were dropped. This is how the raids were often chronicled on individual aircraft, together with decorations gained by crew members

Centre left: First used in action in March 1942, the Lancaster spearheaded the night bomber offensive and went on to serve Bomber Command for more than ten years. It was the only wartime aircraft to carry Barnes Wallis's 22,000-lb (9,980-kg) Grand Slam bomb

Right: First of the RAF four-engined 'heavies' of the second World War to be used in action, the Short Stirling had a sufficiently heavy armament to operate over France by day as well as night throughout 1941

One of two Lancasters which survive in an airworthy condition in the UK, this B Mk 1 (PA474) would have joined 'Tiger Force' for an offensive against Japan had the war continued. Instead it was used for six years by No 82 (Photo Reconnaissance) Squadron before switching to research work. Refurbished in wartime colours, it flies regularly from RAF Waddington

THE ALLIED BOMBER OFFENSIVE

DURING THE FIRST World War there were several visionaries who saw in the bombing aeroplane a more potent weapon than those being used for battlefield and tactical activity. Few were better placed than Hugh Trenchard, one of the earliest Army aviators, who had been in military aviation in Britain from its inception. He put forward ideas for the strategic use of aircraft for bombing and, before the war was over, had been asked to form and command the Independent Force, an organisation within the newly-established Royal Air Force with the specific task of employing aircraft in a strategic role.

After the war the Royal Air Force, under Trenchard's guidance, grew up with a strong traditional belief that 'the best form of defence is attack' and that this attack should pre-eminently be strategic bombing. Bomber Command was formed for this primary purpose in the 1930s, when the RAF expanded to meet the threat of the Luftwaffe, and when the second World War started it was anxious to put its theories into practice. The Command was divided into five groups, two with light/medium bombers (Battles and Blenheims) and three with medium/heavy bombers (Whitleys, Hampdens and Wellingtons). A sizeable portion of the light bomber force was hived off straight away to form part of the RAF's forces in France, committed to tactical support of the armies.

Bomber Command opened its offensive with unbounded confidence, but was hedged in by restrictions which impeded the flexibility of its operation. To avoid incurring a full blitzkrieg on this country it was decided that bombers would not fly over Germany nor drop bombs on any but strictly military installations. Within this limitation Bomber Command immediately went on to the offensive, remaining true to the tenet of attack, by sending aircraft out over the North Sea against German Navy installations. A force of Blenheims, sent off for a late afternoon attack on ships in Heligoland Bight, met atrocious weather conditions and the mission was ineffective. Fourteen Wellingtons, attempting the same task in the Wilhelmshafen area, lost two of their number for little result. On the bigger bombers, the Air Ministry practice of arming the aircraft with several gun positions and/or turrets was soon found to be insufficient for daylight operations, and these tentative raids were abandoned.

The next move was to send Whitley squadrons roaming over Germany during the long winter nights, dropping nothing more fearsome than leaflets. They met little opposition: in fact the bombers' fiercest opponent was the winter weather; but little was accomplished apart from the training value to the crews of getting to know their way about Germany at night. This kid-glove approach was maintained all through the 'Phoney War', partly for political reasons and partly because Bomber Command had not yet acquired sufficient resources to mount a sustained offensive. But after the invasion of the Low Countries and France, Bomber Command was im-

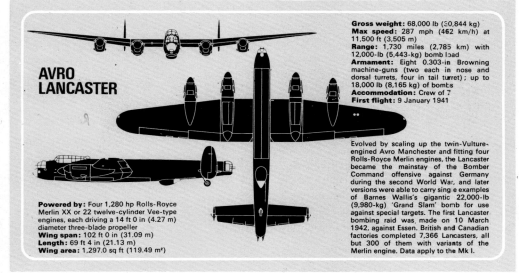

AVRO LANCASTER

Gross weight: 68,000 lb (30,844 kg)
Max speed: 287 mph (462 km/h) at 11,500 ft (3,505 m)
Range: 1,730 miles (2,785 km) with 12,000-lb (5,443-kg) bomb load
Armament: Eight 0.303-in Browning machine-guns (two each in nose and dorsal turrets, four in tail turret); up to 18,000 lb (8,165 kg) of bombs
Accommodation: Crew of 7
First flight: 9 January 1941

Evolved by scaling up the twin-Vulture-engined Avro Manchester and fitting four Rolls-Royce Merlin engines, the Lancaster became the mainstay of the Bomber Command offensive against Germany during the second World War, and later versions were able to carry single examples of Barnes Wallis's gigantic 22,000-lb (9,980-kg) 'Grand Slam' bomb for use against special targets. The first Lancaster bombing raid was made on 10 March 1942, against Essen. British and Canadian factories completed 7,366 Lancasters, all but 300 of them with variants of the Merlin engine. Data apply to the Mk I.

Powered by: Four 1,280 hp Rolls-Royce Merlin XX or 22 twelve-cylinder Vee-type engines, each driving a 14 ft 0 in (4.27 m) diameter three-blade propeller
Wing span: 102 ft 0 in (31.09 m)
Length: 69 ft 4 in (21.13 m)
Wing area: 1,297.0 sq ft (119.49 m²)

Above: 'Bombing up' a Stirling. Because its bomb-bay was divided into sections, the largest weapon this bomber could carry was a 4,000-pounder. More often it carried a heavy load of smaller bombs, as illustrated

Opposite page, top left: One of the biggest problems faced by Germany's night fighter force was to try to intercept the Mosquito light bomber. Able to outfly the opposition, even when carrying a 4,000-lb (1,814-kg) bomb, de Havilland's 'Wooden Wonder' had sufficient range to attack Berlin night after night

Centre left: 'Your vegetables will be planted here.' Bomber Command Stirling crews being briefed for a minelaying mission, known as 'gardening'. Mines laid by the RAF sank 759 German-controlled ships, totalling 721,977 tons, in north-west European waters

Top right: Some of the 800 craters left by a Bomber Command raid on Volkel airfield in Holland on 3 September 1944

Bottom: The railway viaduct at Bielefeld, which carried the main line between Hamm and Hannover, photographed three days after an attack with 22,000-lb (9,980-kg) and 12,000-lb (5,443-kg) bombs by Lancasters of No 617 ('Dam-busters') Squadron on 14 March 1945. The structure remains wrecked to this day

This page, top: Halifax tugs, Horsa and Hamilcar gliders, on the eve of the D-Day invasion of Europe, 6 June 1944. The bombers used for this task retained their full attack capability

mediately thrown into action tactically, bombing behind the enemy lines to relieve pressure on the battlefield.

Even after the fall of France, during which the Command's contingent on the continent was virtually wiped out, bombers from the UK maintained what offensive they could against the enemy air forces and the build-up of invasion forces. Blenheims by day and 'heavies' by night mounted small-scale raids over the nearer Continental airfields and ports. The Command also attacked some strategic targets, principally oil installations. When the immediate danger to Britain ended at the close of September 1940, the Air Staff lost no time in organising a proper strategic bombing policy.

There was a strong and natural desire on the part of Londoners to 'have a crack' at Berlin, but the Air Staff wisely decided that all attacks were to be against precise objectives rather than degenerate into area bombing. The two techniques were combined on the night of 24/25 September 1940, when a force of 119 bombers was mustered to attack gas-works and power stations in Berlin. From then on, the night offensive slowly developed, with oil plants at top priority. Even so, forces were time and again diverted to fulfil more immediate needs, particularly at the behest of the Admiralty, whose own situation was becoming increasingly fraught. This continued into 1941, the ports on the French west coast becoming particularly familiar to Bomber Command crews. In 1941

Stirling four-engined bombers—the first of the real 'heavies'—began to take their effective place in Bomber Command's armoury. They were tried out initially by day but proved no better suited to such operations than the Hampdens, Whitleys and Wellingtons before them, and before long were used solely at night.

During 1941 the move towards area bombing made itself felt. It had many protagonists in Bomber Command, for it was realised increasingly that many of the attacks being made against precision targets were wasteful, in that a high proportion of the bombs were falling outside—some well outside—the target area, resulting in negligible damage. So targets were chosen more and more on the basis of being within an environment which was worth attacking anyway. Targets within an industrial town, for example, would be more favoured than isolated pinpoint targets elsewhere. By this means many towns in Germany were attacked regularly, as well as the particular targets within them.

In the summer of 1941 the bomber offensive strode ahead. Pressure was off the Command to waste its energy on keeping ships in port at Brest, and help from the boffins had arrived to assist the bomber crews with navigational accuracy. This took the form of 'Gee', a radio navigational aid which was the forerunner of a whole series of radio and radar devices that put the bomber offensive ahead of its German opposition. The force, now consisting of nearly 1,000 bombers, was redirected in

July 1941 against the main rail centres of the Reich, with the intention of so dislocating the transportation system as to afford maximum assistance to the Russians. Secondary (on paper at least) was the attack against large centres of industrial population in order to disrupt production of essential means of waging war. More and more, however, this became the real motive behind the offensive, with the intention of wearing down the German population as a whole, not simply by mass murder, but rather by the wholesale destruction of their amenities and services.

The Ruhr valley figured prominently in this offensive, and became the battleground over which bombers fought their fiercest and bloodiest battles—for the defences of the Ruhr were soon so built-up that the area became an almost impregnable fortress. The results were reflected by an increase in Bomber Command's casualties, and as 1941 drew to a close its activities tailed off in order to conserve energies for a spring offensive.

This was officially implemented in February 1942, and was to make use of increasing numbers of aircraft equipped with Gee, before a counter to it was found by the Luftwaffe. To relieve the Russians as much as possible and to pave a way for a second front, the objective was to destroy the morale of the civilian population, particularly the industrial workers. The views of Bomber Command's new Commander-in-Chief, Air Marshal A T Harris, on strategic bomber operation coincided with this directive. His total force then consisted of approximately 600 aircraft and, though this number remained fairly constant throughout the year, 1942 saw the steady replacement of old twin-engined bombers by the new generation of heavies, and the introduction of Bomber Command's two finest bombers, the Avro Lancaster and D.H. Mosquito. Two other factors which added to the power and effectiveness of the bomber offensive appeared in 1942, although their full import was really not effective until the following year. These were the formation of the Pathfinder Force within Bomber Command and the arrival of the first elements of the US Eighth Air Force at bases in Britain.

It was also a year for learning. Bomber Command was adept at analysing its results, and particularly its failures, in order to learn from them. More and more reliance was placed on incendiary bombs, particularly against towns known to be high fire risks—such as Lubeck, which was devastated at the end of March. With the Lancaster another attempt was made at daylight raiding in force with a daring attack on Augsburg in April; but it was a relatively unsuccessful operation and gave no promise of an easy opening to a round-the-clock offensive. Against this gloomy prognostication came the fresh young Americans and their Flying Fortresses during the summer of 1942, eager to show what they could do with bombers armed to the teeth and carrying the Norden bombsight with which they claimed they could

'drop bombs into a pickle barrel from four miles up'. They were trained for daylight operations only, and came in for an awful savaging from German fighters, as sage old heads at the Air Ministry had forecast. But, to their credit, with immense courage they and their successors stuck at it until they had forged a mighty daylight force which, with the RAF's night offensive, produced the desired round-the-clock offensive which eventually helped to force Germany to surrender.

In 1943 the plan began to come true. The previous year had seen the start of Harris's great thousand-bomber raids, the first on Cologne on 30 May, but these were procured by extraordinary means, using many trainee crews; the normal level of operation had been about 200 aircraft. Now the New Year saw the British and US bomber forces working on complementary lines under terms agreed at the Casablanca conference. The highest-priority target for both forces was the German aircraft industry, with the Eighth Air Force attempting precision raids by daylight and the RAF making area attacks by night on towns concerned with the ancillary industries. Beyond these priorities were a host of other targets worked out at lower levels. At last Bomber Command felt ready and equipped for the task at hand. Its face was set resolutely at that toughest of targets, the Ruhr, and all its energies were bent towards destruction

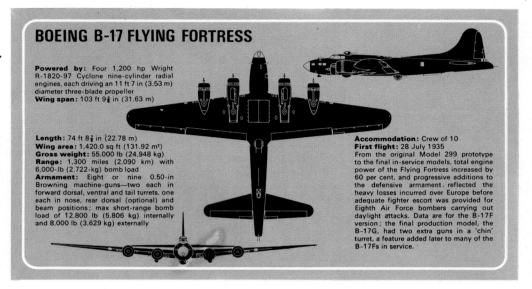

BOEING B-17 FLYING FORTRESS

Powered by: Four 1,200 hp Wright R-1820-97 Cyclone nine-cylinder radial engines, each driving an 11 ft 7 in (3.53 m) diameter three-blade propeller
Wing span: 103 ft 9⅜ in (31.63 m)

Length: 74 ft 8⅝ in (22.78 m)
Wing area: 1,420.0 sq ft (131.92 m²)
Gross weight: 55,000 lb (24,948 kg)
Range: 1,300 miles (2,090 km) with 6,000-lb (2,722-kg) bomb load
Armament: Eight or nine 0.50-in Browning machine-guns—two each in forward dorsal, ventral and tail turrets, one each in nose, rear dorsal (optional) and beam positions; max short-range bomb load of 12,800 lb (5,806 kg) internally and 8,000 lb (3,629 kg) externally

Accommodation: Crew of 10
First flight: 28 July 1935
From the original Model 299 prototype to the final in-service models, total engine power of the Flying Fortress increased by 60 per cent, and progressive additions to the defensive armament reflected the heavy losses incurred over Europe before adequate fighter escort was provided for Eighth Air Force bombers carrying out daylight attacks. Data are for the B-17F version; the final production model, the B-17G, had two extra guns in a 'chin' turret, a feature added later to many of the B-17Fs in service.

Top right: While Bomber Command hammered Europe at night, with its four-engined 'heavies', the US Eighth Air Force completed the 'round-the-clock' offensive in daylight. Staggering losses were incurred initially, until defensive armament and armouring were improved, and escort fighters with sufficient range to accompany the bombers all the way to the target and back were introduced into service. Mainstay of the American bomber force was the Boeing B-17G Flying Fortress; 8,680 of this version were produced by Douglas, Lockheed and Boeing themselves, with 16 coming off the assembly lines at Boeing's Seattle plant every 24 hours

Right: The scale of B-17 production at Seattle is well illustrated in this picture released in 1942, just after America entered the war. Altogether, 12,731 Flying Fortresses were built, a 'big bomber' production total exceeded only by the Convair B-24 Liberator

Far right: At least 49 Flying Fortresses are known to survive world-wide, including this one at the US Air Force Museum, Wright-Patterson Air Force Base, Dayton, Ohio

Centre right: The B-17G had no fewer than thirteen 50-calibre guns to ensure a hail of cross-fire when a formation of Fortresses came under attack. Their positions are indicated in this diagram, which shows the new chin turret introduced on the 'G'. In an attempt to produce a really heavily-armed escort aircraft, 21 Fortresses were modified into B-40s, carrying up to 30 machine-guns and cannon; but these were not successful

Bottom right: Part of the wonderful mosaic ceiling by Francis Scott Bradford at the memorial to men of the US armed forces who died in the second World War, at Madingley, near Cambridge. Dedicated to men of the USAAF, the ceiling shows their aircraft, each type clearly recognisable. The parts of the mosaic in deep blue denote the depth of infinity; the lighter colours reflect the light of Heaven breaking through the earthly layers of the sky, with a lighter nimbus surrounding each aircraft to separate it from earthly forces as it makes its final flight of the area. But first it had to dispose of an old distraction—the U-boat ports on the French west coast, which were again causing the Navy great trouble. By now further aids were forthcoming: 'Oboe' was first used in March 1943, and the Pathfinder Force was becoming a really economical and devastating means of leading an attack.

This was the year, too, in which the Americans' great bombing fleet was blooded in only too literal a way. Pursuing their intention of massed daylight assaults on Germany brought to the Fortress and Liberator crews a succession of distressing and costly enterprises and they were obliged to fly under the protection of a fighter umbrella. But when they were so escorted

the American raids became far more effective and casualties were reduced to an acceptable level. At first British Spitfires were used as escort, but these had barely enough range for the task; later the American bombers had an escort force comprising their own P-38 Lightnings, P-47 Thunderbolts and (later) P-51 Mustangs. From that moment, the Eighth Air Force was truly in business, and by early 1944 exceeded Bomber Command in numbers.

The pattern was now set, and it remained only for the two forces, side by side, to step up their fearsome offensive until the Reich was defeated. In the process, several other refinements were introduced. Many of these were of a 'black box' nature, not only

providing the bombers with better navigation and bombing aids but helping them to dislocate the German night-fighter and other defensive organisations. A whole Group was built up within Bomber Command whose express purpose was the complete dislocation of the German defensive machine by radio and radar devices. Very effective it was, too, operating 'spoof' raids and sending alternative transmissions on the German control frequencies, with bogus orders to the night-fighter crews, who could never be sure whether they were hearing friend or foe.

In 1944 the attention of both day and night bomber forces was turned increasingly towards the installations which had sprung up across the Channel, from which the German Vergeltungswaffen (reprisal weapons) were to be launched against the UK. But by April a more vital task had dawned, and for some months the whole vast weight of the two forces was put at the disposal of the Supreme Allied Commander in Europe for support of the invasion of Europe. By then such ascendancy had been gained over the Luftwaffe that Allied losses by day were on the wane, and henceforth Bomber Command's heavies came out increasingly by day, providing their own 24-hour offensive. Their well-tried methods of attack underwent increasing sophistication, and outsize bombs like the 'Tallboy' and 'Grand Slam' began to appear on specially-modified Lancasters.

When the invasion forces were established so firmly on Continental soil as to need no further backing from the heavies, Bomber Command and the Eighth Air Force returned to the attack on Germany itself. Again the principal target was oil: if Germany's oil plants could be severely hit. the Luftwaffe would be rendered impotent and the Wehrmacht made immobile. Backing this up were attacks on other transportation systems; 'Bomber' Harris made sure that the RAF's contribution was flown in terms of area attacks where they would most demoralise, and specialised squadrons, using principally Mosquitos, were trained for raids on pinpoint targets.

The stranglehold which this final devastating offensive had on Germany began to make itself felt early in 1945. The writing was on the wall, and it was only a matter of time before the heavy blows which American and British forces alike were raining on Germany took their full effect. Never before had such a huge force of men and machines been built up, skilled in experience and terrible in execution. The protagonists of aerial bombardment had been vindicated in awful fashion.

AIR WAR OVER AFRICA

THE ENTRY OF ITALY into the second World War found the British in the Middle East dangerously weak both in the air and on the ground. A few squadrons of Gladiator fighter biplanes and Blenheim twin-engined bombers faced a much larger force of the Italian Regia Aeronautica, equipped with aircraft of similar vintage—Fiat C.R.42 fighter biplanes and Savoia-Marchetti S.M.79 tri-motor bombers. The RAF took the offensive early, attacking Italian airfields in Libya during the first days of the war; but although Italian troops finally advanced over the frontier into Egypt in September 1940, they stopped after a few miles and a stalemate ensued until December. Then, with a far smaller but very efficient mobile force, and with his air strength reinforced by a few Hurricane fighters, General Wavell launched a limited offensive which quickly grew to an all-out push as the vastly larger Italian army retreated across Cyrencaica to the borders of Tripolitania.

Here the British had to halt, due to the shortage of supplies and the long lines of communication; but by this time the RAF had virtually driven the Regia Aeronautica from the skies, and the Hurricanes ruled supreme. Unfortunately, it was at this juncture that the RAF was greatly weakened by the despatch of a number of squadrons to the aid of the Greeks, while at the same time Rommel's Afrika Korps began arriving in Tripoli, bringing with it elements of the Luftwaffe straight from the Battle of Britain and equipped with modern Messerschmitt Bf 109 and 110 fighters, and Junkers Ju 87 dive-bombers.

Late in March 1941 Rommel launched a probing attack on the critically-weakened British positions, and in a few weeks had sent the Imperial forces reeling back right across the Egyptian frontier, the Luftwaffe gaining a considerable ascendancy at this time. While this was happening, apart from the squadrons sent to Greece, RAF and South African units were also fighting the Italians over East Africa; but by May the fighting there was almost over, and the evacuation of Greece and Crete had been completed. The arrival of some reinforcements allowed a small offensive—Operation 'Brevity'—to be undertaken, but this was an immediate failure. Following some fighting with insurrectionists in Iraq, the Vichy French colony of Syria was occupied in July, but not without hard fighting with the garrison forces both on the ground and in the air. By this time, too, the arrival of units released from East Africa and the receipt of such American aircraft as the Curtiss Tomahawk fighter and Martin Maryland bomber provided the opportunity for a further limited offensive, launched in June and known as Operation 'Battleaxe'; this had no more success than 'Brevity'.

A period of consolidation followed, during which time the Western Desert Air Force, as it was now known, was greatly reinforced. This period lasted until November 1941 when an all-out offensive, code-named 'Crusader', was mounted to drive the Axis out of Cyrenaica and to relieve the port of Tobruk, which had been under siege since April. Blenheims, Marylands, Hurricanes and Tomahawks by day, and

Wellingtons by night, hammered at the German and Italian forces and fought the Luftwaffe and Regia Aeronautica in the air as General Auchinleck's troops advanced once more to the borders of Tripolitania in a long, hard-fought battle. The WDAF won a degree of superiority in the air which it never again lost, and which increased with every month that passed. Ju 87s, Bf 110s and Italian aircraft were shot from the skies in furious air battles, though the relatively small number of Bf 109s remained superior to anything the British could put into the air. Too small in numbers now to challenge seriously the growing strength of the WDAF, they kept up a series of sniping attacks on its formations which maintained a rate of loss far higher than the RAF was to suffer in any of its other tactical air forces. It was in attacks of this nature that the legendary German fighter pilot, Hans-Joachim Marseille, was to shoot down the greatest number of British aircraft claimed by any pilot of either war—151 in eighteen months!

At the turn of the year the forces in the Middle East were again weakened when units were withdrawn and reinforcements re-routed to the Far East, where the Japanese had just attacked. Rommel picked this moment to repeat his probing attack of the previous year; catching the Imperial forces off balance, he sent them back across Cyrenaica once more. This time the retreat stopped about half-way to the Egyptian frontier on the Gazala Line, and here stalemate was again the order of the day for several months.

Left: Pilots of the RAF's Western Desert Air Force with their Spitfire V fighters

Right: Abandoned in the path of a British advance, this Fiat C.R.42 fighter of the Regia Aeronautica has already begun to attract souvenir hunters, as the hole in the fabric covering of its rear fuselage testifies

Centre: Tomahawks, Kittyhawks and Warhawks of the Curtiss P-40 family were never outstanding as fighting machines, but played their part in the victories over North Africa

Bottom: Martin Baltimores gave fine service by day and night with light bomber squadrons of the Desert Air Force, during the North African offensive and in the subsequent advance through Italy. This one, 'R-for-Redwing', has 80 operations recorded on its nose

1940-43

FIAT C.R.42

Powered by: One 840 hp Fiat A.74R.1C 38 fourteen-cylinder radial engine, driving a 9 ft 2¼ in (2.80 m) diameter three-blade propeller
Wing span: 31 ft 10 in (9.70 m)
Length: 27 ft 1¼ in (8.26 m)
Wing area: 241.1 sq ft (22.40 m²)
Gross weight: 5,033 lb (2,283 kg)
Max speed: 267 mph (430 km/h) at 17,490 ft (5,330 m)
Normal range: 482 miles (775 km)
Armament: Two 12.7-mm machine-guns in upper front fuselage; two similar guns or two 220-lb (100-kg) bombs beneath lower wings

Accommodation: Crew of 1
First flight: early 1939
The Falco, as the C.R.42 was known to the Italian Air Force, was the last of a long line of *Caccia* (fighter) *Rosatelli* biplane fighters produced by the Fiat company during the inter-war years. Although the C.R.42 was an excellent example of its genre, the combat value of the fighter biplane in a monoplane age was dramatically highlighted by the Falco's record: Italy entered the war with 143 of these aircraft, a total of 1,781 was eventually built, yet by the time of the Italian surrender in September 1943 only 113 survived.

into retreat again, the British forces withdrew across the Egyptian frontier, this time losing Tobruk, and the Afrika Korps reached its high water mark when the 8th Army finally stopped on a prepared line at El Alamein. Throughout July the army held on while the air force threw everything into stopping the Axis advance, including the first Spitfires to arrive in the desert, Hurricane 'tank-busters' with anti-tank guns beneath their wings, Kittyhawks carrying 250-lb (113-kg) and 500-lb (227-kg) bombs, and Beaufighters. Between army and air force, the line was held.

At this time the first American air units arrived to support the British, and P-40 Warhawks, B-24 Liberators and B-25 Mitchells were soon flying alongside the Australian, British and South African squadrons of the WDAF. In early September Rommel again tried to breach the Allied line, but his attack was swiftly beaten off, mainly by air power. By the following month the WDAF had reached its zenith, and though its fighters and fighter-bombers continued to suffer grievous losses to the marauding Messerschmitts, the bombers always got through to destroy stores and supply

dumps, shatter aircraft on the ground and generally demoralise the enemy.

Late in October General Bernard Montgomery, who had taken over command of the 8th Army after the retreat from Gazala, launched his great Alamein offensive, and after a week of slogging, the Axis forces broke and fled westwards, their packed columns the target of continual air attack. As the opposing armies flowed once more to the west, across the Cyrenaican desert, British and American forces, supported by carriers of both the US and Royal Navies, landed in Morocco and Algeria, far in Rommel's rear. Little resistance was met on the ground, but a short, savage battle was fought with the Vichy French in the air. Units of the RAF with Spitfires, Hurricanes and Bisleys, and of the USAAF, also with Spitfires, and with P-40s, P-38 Lightnings and A-20 Havocs, quickly moved in, and the Allies pushed eastwards towards Tunisia. The Axis high command in the Mediterranean acted with commendable speed, flying both ground and air forces into Tunisia just in time to hold the British 1st Army in the mountains west of Bizerta as the winter set in.

At first, with good bases close to the front, the Axis enjoyed air superiority over Tunisia, but the Allies were steadily reinforced throughout late 1942/early 1943 with B-17 Flying Fortresses, B-25 and B-26 medium bombers, and new Spitfire IXs, and many hard-fought actions took place. To the south the 8th Army took Tripoli in January and moved up to the Tunisian border. In February, feeling momentarily safe behind the Mareth Line, which blocked entry into southern Tunisia, Rommel struck north-westwards against the American and French troops in his rear at the Battle of Kasserine Pass, inflicting heavy losses both in the air and on the ground, and nearly succeeded in breaking the Allied front completely. His thrust was finally held, and in March Montgomery attacked his now-weakened forces at Mareth, outflanking the line and sending the Afrika Korps once more into retreat.

By early April the Allied armies had linked, and began compressing the Axis into northern Tunisia. During this month frantic efforts were made to supply the Axis troops by great fleets of transport aircraft from Sicily. Allied fighters patrolled their flight paths and shot them down literally in hundreds. Against the first American daylight raids by four-engined bombers, escorted by long-range fighters, and the ever-growing Allied air power over every corner of their territory, some of the best fighter pilots of the Luftwaffe from both Eastern and Western fronts fought desperately, but in vain; by early May they had to withdraw to Sicily, their bases in Africa no longer tenable. By this time the Allies had begun a final thrust all along the front. In overwhelming numerical superiority, with Allied air power now absolutely supreme, they steadily eliminated the Axis forces, the last resistance ending on the Cap Bon peninsula on 13 May 1943, just under three years since the war in Africa had begun.

The power and vigilance of the RAF and USAAF prevented the possibility of any evacuation to Sicily, and nearly a quarter of a million prisoners were taken, together with quantities of weapons, supplies, etc. In three years the Allied air forces had grown from a tiny contingent to a mighty weapon on which the army had come to rely greatly. Many lessons had been learnt in co-operation, and the Western Desert Air Force was to be the model on which the Allied tactical air forces were based for the rest of the war. Against heat, all-enveloping dust, flies, shortage of water and supplies, and against great odds, the men of the Commonwealth air forces, and later of the USAAF, had carried on and had won. The airmen of the Luftwaffe and Regia Aeronautica had fought bravely and well, and had gained many tactical successes; but they had failed, despite their opportunities, to forge their air forces into a compact whole with a common objective as the British and Americans had done.

Opposite page, top to bottom: On 11 June 1940, the first day of the East African campaign, Vickers Wellesleys destroyed 350,000 gallons (1,591,000 litres) of petrol on the Eritrean airfield of Massawa. They carried bombs in underwing canisters

One of ten Junkers Ju 87 dive-bombers, manned by Italians, which force-landed on or near the British side of the front line in North Africa, to the amazement of the local troops

Fresh from its victory in the Battle of Britain, the Spitfire followed its partner, the Hurricane, to new successes as Rommel's Afrika Korps was driven out of Cyrenaica, then Tripolitania and finally Tunisia

Returning from a low-level attack on enemy tanks, a Hurricane pilot gets a friendly wave from British anti-aircraft gunners

The wreckage of a Fiat G.50 fighter reflects the sad ending of Mussolini's grandiose plan to ride into Alexandria in triumph after clearing the British from North Africa

This page, left: First American bombers used by the RAF in North Africa were Martin Marylands. Their most famous operation was a reconnaissance of the Italian fleet at Taranto before the devastating Fleet Air Arm attack with Swordfish biplanes on 11 November 1940

Below: North American B-25 bombers of the USAAF were among the types which helped to end enemy air superiority over Tunisia in the Winter of 1942/43

Air War in the Pacific 1941-45

ON 7 DECEMBER 1941 a powerful force of Japanese carrier aircraft struck at Pearl Harbor, the American naval base in the Hawaiian Islands, and in a devastating surprise attack destroyed or damaged a large part of the US fleet. On the other side of the International Date Line, on 8 December, but in fact at the same time, the Japanese army invaded Malaya, while land-based naval aircraft raided American airfields in the Philippines. Japan had entered the second World War with a rush!

At once the western Allies were made painfully aware that the previously-derided Japanese technology had turned out warplanes which were in many ways superior to anything they possessed. It had also produced a powerful fleet, built around the fast aircraft carrier, and Japanese personnel were both highly trained and, to a large extent, already blooded in four years of fighting over China. The Americans were unprepared, the British Empire forces were already fully committed against the Germans and Italians in Europe and the Middle East. Such forces as were available were poorly-equipped and had little proper training for the task now on hand.

The greatest hope for the Allies lay in the fact that all US aircraft carriers were absent from Pearl Harbor at the time of the attack. The British had a small but powerful fleet at Singapore, formed around the modern capital ships *Prince of Wales* and *Repulse*. However, the latter had no adequate air cover, a factor which was to cost them their existence when they sortied to attack Japanese invasion forces landing in eastern Malaya. A force of JNAF twin-engined torpedo-bombers flew unescorted from French Indo-China to attack at maximum range and succeeded in sinking both British warships.

The brightest star in the Japanese arsenal was the Navy's Mitsubishi Zero fighter, and this, together with the Army's Nakajima fighters, quickly cut a swathe through the Brewster Buffalos, Seversky P-35s, Curtiss Hawks and P-40s of the defending British, Australian, New Zealand, Dutch and American air forces. Reinforcements of British Hurricanes and later-model American P-40s were rushed out, but could do little, and in rapid succession Malaya, Singapore, Borneo, the Dutch East Indies and the Philippines fell to the invaders.

Only in Burma was the picture marginally brighter; here the RAF defenders were joined by the Tomahawks of the American Volunteer Group—the 'Flying Tigers'—experienced pilots trained by Colonel Claire Chennault, air adviser to the Chinese Nationalists, in special tactics devised by him from experience of fighting the Japanese over the previous three years. Early raids on Rangoon were decimated, and for a while brought to a halt, by these fighters. With the fall of Malaya, however, an invasion of Burma began and the British were driven inexorably back into India. The Allied air units put up a splendid fight before losing most of their remaining aircraft on the ground in March 1942, and by the end of that month Burma also was in Japanese hands.

The Japanese carrier fleet, fresh from its triumph at Pearl Harbor, had rampaged through the East Indies, and had launched an attack on the north-west Australian port of Darwin. Then, early in April, it pushed into the Indian Ocean and, unable to bring the British Eastern Fleet to battle, struck at Colombo and Trincomalee on the island of Ceylon. At both ports determined RAF fighter opposition was met, and little damage was done; but out to sea the small aircraft carrier HMS *Hermes* was spotted and sunk, as were two cruisers. This was the first time a carrier had been sunk by carrier-based aircraft, and the Japanese were understandably jubilant.

By May 1942 the Japanese advance was reaching its high-water mark. In the south forces had landed in northern New Guinea; an effort was next made to land a further force on the south-east coast of the island, and a section of the carrier fleet sped to the Coral Sea to support this. American carriers were in the area, spotted the Japanese first, and the first naval battle fought entirely by aircraft ensued. It ended virtually in a draw, each side losing one carrier, with a second badly damaged. However, the Japanese ships were forced to withdraw and the invasion of south-east New Guinea was then repulsed by Australian troops and Kittyhawk fighters.

A month later almost the whole of the Japanese fleet set sail to capture the island of Midway, which was defended by a small force of US Marine Corps aircraft. They attacked the island, decimating the defending Marine Buffalos, and then cut to pieces attacks launched by USMC and USAAF bombers against the massive concentration of shipping. An American force of only three carriers (all that were available) was rushed to the area, and by luck the Japanese

Right: The Republic P-47 Thunderbolt was another US fighter which was flown very successfully by the British services. These Thunderbolts of No 135 Squadron were photographed at an airstrip on the Arakan front in Burma, in November 1944

Far right, top: The sharply cranked wing of the Corsair enabled the undercarriage to be kept quite short despite the large diameter of the propeller

Far right, bottom: Despite troubles with its 1,900 hp Homare Ha-45 engine, the Nakajima Ki-84-Ia Hayate (Gale) was one of the few Japanese fighters able to hold their own against US Hellcats, Mustangs and Thunderbolts in the last year of the war. Instead of the former Japanese emphasis on manoeuvrability at all costs, it introduced better armour protection for the pilot and self-sealing fuel tanks

Opposite page: Mitsubishi Ki-21s were the standard heavy bombers of the Japanese Army Air Force at the time of the attack on Pearl Harbor, having served earlier in the war against China. These Ki-21-IIs could carry a 2,200-lb (1,000 kg) bomb-load

Left: Among other operational types produced by Mitsubishi was the Ki-46-III reconnaissance aircraft. Known to the Allies as 'Dinah' it was one of the most elegant aeroplanes of the second World War

Below: Chance Vought's F4U Corsair was considered by the US Navy to be too fast for carrier operations, until the Royal Navy had taken it to sea and proved its outstanding qualities as a deck fighter. As a result, America used it initially to equip hard-hitting Marine squadrons land-based in places like Bougainville

Left: Kawasaki's Ki-61 Hien (Flying Swallow) fighter had rather Germanic lines as a result of the installation of a licence-built Daimler-Benz DB 601 engine. Although one of the most effective weapons used against high-flying US Superfortress bombers, such attacks often cost the lives of Japanese pilots who rammed their targets rather than relying on guns. This Ki-61-Ic was pressed into post-war service by the Chinese Air Force

Right: Japan's first jet aircraft, the Nakajima J8N1 Kikka (Sacred Blossom), flew for the first time on 7 August 1945, one day after the first atomic bomb had dropped on Hiroshima

Far right: One of the finest fighters of the Pacific War, the Kawanishi N1K2-J Shiden (Violet Lightning) was evolved from the N1K1 Kyofu floatplane. This one survives in the USAF Museum at Wright-Patterson Air Force Base

Below: Firefighters busy on board HMS *Formidable* after a Japanese *Kamikaze* suicide aircraft crashed into the flight deck. Such attacks caused only temporary damage to steel-decked British carriers, but sank several wooden-decked US ships

Bottom: Most suicide attacks by Japanese pilots were made in standard types of combat aircraft. Exceptions were those carried out in specially-designed rocket-powered Yokosuka MXY-7 Ohka (Cherry Blossom) piloted bombs, like this captured example. The Ohka was air-launched from a Mitsubishi G4M2e mother-plane

were again spotted first. Strikes were launched and a force of Douglas Devastator torpedo-planes bored in at low level. They were attacked by fighters and the guns of every vessel in the fleet, and were massacred to the last aircraft—but they were the undoing of the Japanese. As every element of the defence was concentrating on the torpedo-bombers, flying just above the waves, Douglas Dauntless dive-bombers appeared from the clouds directly overhead and plummeted on to the unsuspecting carriers, inflicting terrible damage. The Japanese later got off a retaliatory strike which sank the American carrier *Yorktown;* but at the end of the day no fewer than four Japanese carriers had gone down. It was the turning point of the war in the Pacific.

A period of recoupment on both sides now took place, the USAAF and Royal Australian Air Force settling down to the start of a long war of attrition over New Guinea against JAAF and JNAF air units based on the other side of the island. In October it was noticed that the Japanese had constructed an airstrip on Guadalcanal island in the Central Solomons. This appeared to presage further expansion, and in consequence the first American counter-invasion was launched by Marines to take the island.

This led to heavy activity in the air, as the Japanese fought fanatically to hold on to the island. US Marine Wildcats and Army Airacobras fought off repeated raids by counter-attacking enemy aircraft, operating in appalling conditions in a siege every bit as epic as that on Malta. Violent naval actions around the Solomons erupted in October into the Battle of Santa Cruz, where the Americans came off worst, losing the carrier *Hornet;* but gradually the hold on the island was consolidated and the last flames of resistance were finally quenched.

The only year of the Pacific War which was near to being static was 1943. In the Solomons, Marine Corsairs, Army P-40s and P-38s and New Zealand Kittyhawks arrived to join in a long battle with the garrisons of Japanese air bases in the area. Army Liberators and Marine Dauntlesses struck at targets in New Britain and on other islands. Over New Guinea, too, the fight went on—the Americans sending more modern aircraft, albeit in small numbers, to oppose the highly-manoeuvrable Japanese fighters. The most successful of the US newcomers proved to be the P-38 Lightnings, twin-engined single-seaters.

Japanese bombers had maintained a steady series of raids on the Darwin area of Australia, but early in 1943 a wing of defending Spitfires from England went into action and managed to inflict sufficiently heavy losses to discourage further attacks. Meanwhile the vast industrial power of the United States was finally getting into its stride. New carriers were beginning to roll off the stocks in increasing numbers, while new aircraft such as the Grumman Hellcat fighter, designed in the light of experience with the Zero, the Avenger torpedo-bomber and the Helldiver dive-bomber, were also appearing. The first action by the earliest of the new carriers and Hellcat fighters occurred in August, when they struck at installations on Japanese-held Marcus Island.

Meanwhile, in Burma a British offensive on the Mayu Peninsula had failed early in the year, and in China the Sino-American air forces were not strong enough to do more than hold on. By autumn, however, the RAF and USAAF were able to launch a limited air offensive against the Rangoon area; when the Japanese reciprocated they were met by newly-arrived Spitfires and repulsed in a series of fierce battles which extended over the next four months.

By early 1944 the new American fast carrier task forces which made up the 7th Fleet began operations on a really large scale, opening with a strike on the Marshall Islands during February. The USAAF was also preparing to launch a deadly new weapon—the giant B-29 Superfortress bomber. First bases for the B-29 were built in India, and raids began from there in June. They were the first attacks to be made on

the Japanese mainland since a force of B-25 Mitchells, led by Lt-Col 'Jimmy' Doolittle, had taken off from the carrier *Hornet* in 1942, bombed various targets, and then attempted to fly on to China.

The bases in India were far from ideal, as they confronted the bombers with a long flight over the 'Hump', the range of mountains between Assam and China. To provide bases on islands within striking range of Japan, it was decided to invade Saipan in the Marianas in June 1944. The landings were supported by the 7th Fleet's carrier task force, which hit the area first. The Japanese Navy reacted violently as the invasion went in, enemy carriers approaching and launching a number of large strikes on 19 June. The defending Hellcats intercepted each raid, and in a day known subsequently as the 'Marianas Turkey Shoot', shot down 220 of the 328 aircraft opposing them for minimal losses in return. Next day the Americans hit the Japanese carriers, sinking one and damaging four more, as well as a battleship.

Following the Marianas operations, the US carriers struck at bases in the Philippines in September, inflicting further heavy losses, and then repeated the process against Formosa early in October. Meantime the forces in the south and south-west Pacific, supported by the USAAF, USMC, RAAF and RNZAF, had reconquered New Guinea and either invaded, or by-passed and neutralised from the air, islands in the Solomons chain—a process christened 'island-hopping'.

At last these forces under General Douglas MacArthur were ready to return to the Philippines, and a bold stroke was

CHANCE VOUGHT F4U CORSAIR

Powered by: One 2,100 hp Pratt & Whitney R-2800-18W Double Wasp eighteen-cylinder radial engine, driving a 13 ft 2 in (4.01 m) diameter four-blade propeller
Wing span: 41 ft 0 in (12.50 m)
Length: 33 ft 8 in (10.26 m)
Wing area: 314 sq ft (29.17 m²)
Gross weight: 14,670 lb (6,654 kg)
Max speed: 446 mph (718 km/h) at 26,200 ft (8,535 m)
Range: 1,005 miles (1,617 km)
Armament: Six 0.50-in machine-guns in wings; two 1,000-lb (454-kg) bombs under fuselage
Accommodation: Crew of 1

First flight: 29 May 1940
First production US warplane to exceed 400 mph (644 km/h) in level flight, the Corsair became operational in the Pacific war from February 1943, subsequently serving with units of the US Navy, US Marine Corps, Fleet Air Arm and Royal New Zealand Air Force. Its distinctive engine note and high 'kill ratio' over enemy aircraft quickly earned it the nickname 'Whistling Death' from its Japanese opponents. The data and silhouette apply to the last major wartime variant, the F4U-4, but in all the Corsair remained in production for an 11-year period during which 12,571 of these fighters were built.

Left, top to bottom:
The Aichi M6A Seiran (Mountain Haze) was intended to be launched from the I-400 class of ultra-long-range submarines for an attack on the Panama Canal. In fact it was too late to be used operationally

First and most famous of all American 'sharkmouth' units were the 'Flying Tigers' of the American Volunteer Group who supported the Chinese armies against Japanese invaders. This is one of their Curtiss P-40s

Leading US Marine Corps Corsair 'ace' was Colonel Gregory M 'Pappy' Boyington, who claimed 28 Japanese aircraft destroyed. The flags painted under his cockpit indicate that his 'kills' totalled 20 when this photograph was taken

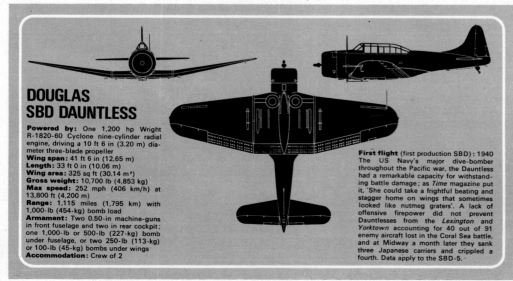

DOUGLAS SBD DAUNTLESS

Powered by: One 1,200 hp Wright R-1820-60 Cyclone nine-cylinder radial engine, driving a 10 ft 6 in (3.20 m) diameter three-blade propeller
Wing span: 41 ft 6 in (12.65 m)
Length: 33 ft 0 in (10.06 m)
Wing area: 325 sq ft (30.14 m²)
Gross weight: 10,700 lb (4,853 kg)
Max speed: 252 mph (406 km/h) at 13,800 ft (4,200 m)
Range: 1,115 miles (1,795 km) with 1,000-lb (454-kg) bomb load
Armament: Two 0.50-in machine-guns in front fuselage and two in rear cockpit; one 1,000-lb or 500-lb (227-kg) bomb under fuselage, or two 250-lb (113-kg) or 100-lb (45-kg) bombs under wings
Accommodation: Crew of 2

First flight (first production SBD): 1940
The US Navy's major dive-bomber throughout the Pacific war, the Dauntless had a remarkable capacity for withstanding battle damage; as *Time* magazine put it, 'She could take a frightful beating and stagger home on wings that sometimes looked like nutmeg graters'. A lack of offensive firepower did not prevent Dauntlesses from the *Lexington* and *Yorktown* accounting for 40 out of 91 enemy aircraft lost in the Coral Sea battle, and at Midway a month later they sank three Japanese carriers and crippled a fourth. Data apply to the SBD-5.

planned to land direct on Luzon, the northern of the main islands. Supported by the fast carriers, by a force of escort carriers, and by the USAAF's 5th and 13th Air Forces to the south, the invasion took place in mid-October. Again the Japanese Navy reacted, sending strong strike forces which surprised the escort carriers supporting the landings in Leyte Gulf and came near to eliminating them. However, the tables were turned and a number of enemy carriers and battleships were sunk, many more aircraft also being shot down.

It was at this time that the first 'Kamikaze' suicide attacks were launched against the US carriers—a form of attack which was to inflict much damage in coming months, and to prove most difficult to combat.

In Burma the Japanese Army had launched its last offensive early in 1944, British forces being isolated in the Arakan, and then at Imphal and Kohima as the Japanese crossed the frontier into India. Supplied, reinforced and supported entirely from the air, the British forces held out while the Japanese exhausted themselves, and then drove them back towards central Burma. Air transport also supplied Chindit columns operating behind the Japanese lines. Following the 1944 monsoon, the British 14th Army began a strong push southwards, again supported and supplied by air. Spitfires, Thunderbolts, Hurricanes, Beaufighters and Mosquitos provided the support, while Dakotas and Commandos carried the supplies, and Liberators struck further afield. By early May 1945 Rangoon had fallen, and only mopping-up remained to be done in Burma.

In January 1945 a British fast carrier task force made a number of strikes on oil targets in the East Indies, taking a heavy toll of the JAAF's defending interceptors, before passing into the Pacific to join the US Navy in operations around the Japanese home islands. The American carriers meantime had pressed into the South China Sea at the start of 1945, striking again at Formosa, and then at targets along the coast of China.

With the availability of the Marianas bases, B-29s had stepped up the raids on Japan from October 1944, creating new problems for the Japanese. The high-flying and powerfully-armed bombers were difficult to intercept, and ever-larger numbers of fighters had to be recalled from overseas to oppose them. The increasing Japanese resistance to the bombers' regular attacks

Top left: In their first clash with Japanese aircraft in New Guinea, pilots of USAAF Lockheed P-38 Lightnings claimed the destruction of 14 'Zeros' without the loss of a single US pilot. One of the 12 P-38s was disabled but the pilot returned to his base

Top right: With special markings painted on its side, a Mitsubishi Ki-57 arrives at Mingaladon Airfield, Rangoon, carrying envoys to sign the Japanese surrender in August 1945

Above: Brewster F2A Buffalo fighters, bought from America, were considered quite suitable for RAF squadrons in the Far East in 1940-41, enabling more potent home-produced fighters to be retained for use against the Germans and Italians. Early experience in combat against the 'Zero' quickly disproved the adequacy of the Buffalo and it was withdrawn from service

Left: Carrying two 1,000-lb bombs and armed with eight 0.50-in machine-guns, a Thunderbolt belonging to the USAAF's 'Burma Banshees' prepares to take off for an attack on Japanese positions

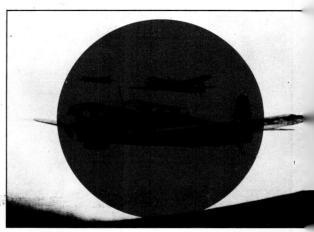

Right: Flight crew members turn the propeller of a C-46 transport at Chenyi in China, prior to a routine operation over the 'Burma Hump'. Flying over high mountain ranges, often in terrible weather, USAAF aircrew kept open this vital supply route from India to their Chinese allies

Far right: The Nakajima B6N1 Tenzan torpedo-bomber was superior in many respects to its Allied counterparts and might have inflicted disastrous blows on US and British naval units in 1944-45 had the Japanese still possessed a large carrier fleet and sufficient skilled pilots

Below: The Martlet fighters and Swordfish torpedo-bombers massed on the flight deck of this British carrier would have formed a tempting target for Japanese *Kamikaze* attack at a later stage of the Pacific War

Bottom: The bomber which brought the Pacific War to an end—the Boeing B-29 Superfortress. Although remembered mainly as the vehicle for America's atomic bombs, the B-29 earlier caused terrible destruction in conventional bombing raids on the Japanese home islands

Left: An RAF Blenheim bomber dives to machine-gun shipping in the harbour at Akyab, a vital Japanese supply centre in Burma

Below: Most successful US Navy dive-bomber of the second World War, the Douglas Dauntless inflicted crippling damage on the Japanese fleet in actions such as the Battle of the Coral Sea, Midway and the Solomons campaign

on their industrial capacity made the provision of long-range fighter escort desirable. So, in February 1945, carrier forces supported the invasion of the island of Iwo Jima, to provide a base for P-51 Mustang fighters for this purpose, as well as a useful emergency landing ground for damaged bombers returning from their targets. In support of the landings the carriers also launched a series of attacks on the Japanese home islands.

Iwo Jima fell after a hard fight. In April the operation was repeated against the island of Okinawa, still closer to Japan, and it was here that the British Pacific Fleet joined the US 7th Fleet. The B-29s meantime had switched in March to night attacks, against which the Japanese had practically no defence. Using area bombing techniques perfected by RAF Bomber Command in Europe, which proved particularly effective against the flimsy structure of most of Japan's buildings, they burned out large areas of the country's major industrial cities in a very short time.

With the Philippines well on the way to being secured, the American and British carriers now operated all around Japan, picking off the remaining vessels of the Japanese Navy and striking at any worthwhile targets remaining on the mainland. Everywhere reconquest was approaching completion, except in China where little progress had been made. All supplies had had to be flown in from India over the 'Hump' route, until the liberation of central Burma reopened the land route, and this prevented a really great concentration of strength ever being achieved—particularly as opportunities elsewhere offered better results for the effort expended.

Much has been made of air power in the European theatre, but it was in the Pacific that its exercise was paramount and decisive in all areas. Now it was to provide the final stroke. Japan's ability to continue the war had been virtually destroyed by July 1945, but still she fought on fanatically. An invasion would clearly be costly in Allied lives, but only one other alternative seemed likely to produce the desired unconditional surrender. On 6 August a B-29 dropped the first atomic bomb on Hiroshima. Two days later the Soviet Union declared war, attacking the Japanese forces based in Manchuria, and next day the second atomic bomb was exploded over Nagasaki. Japan, an outstanding exponent and victim of air power, surrendered on the 14th.

Above and left: Among exhibits at the USAF Museum is the B-29 Superfortress Bockscar from which the second atomic bomb was dropped on Nagasaki, on 9 August 1945, ending the Pacific War

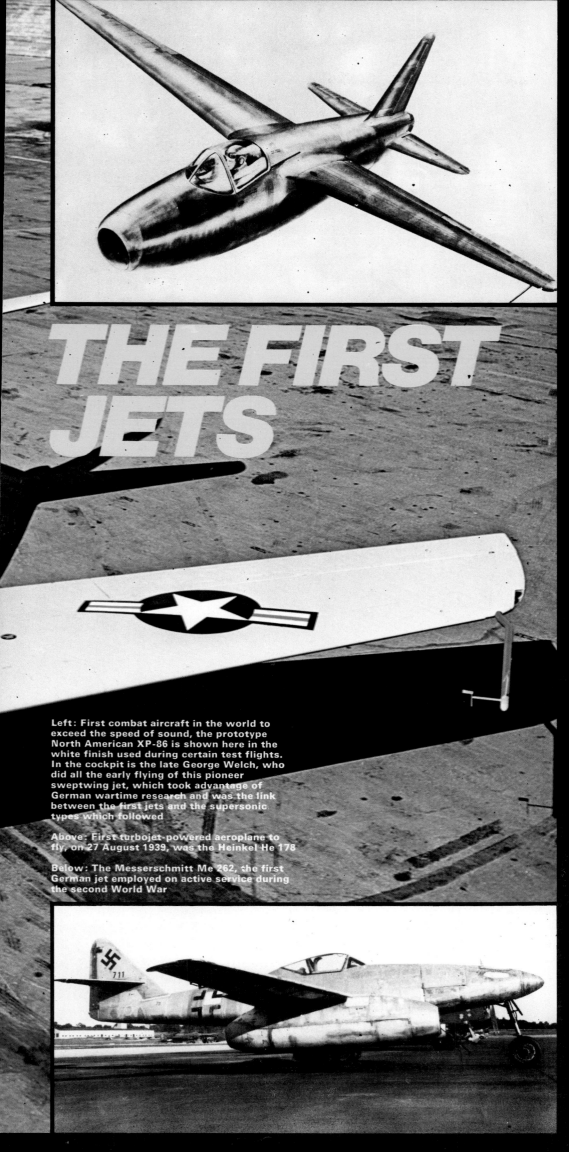

THE FIRST JETS

Left: First combat aircraft in the world to exceed the speed of sound, the prototype North American XP-86 is shown here in the white finish used during certain test flights. In the cockpit is the late George Welch, who did all the early flying of this pioneer sweptwing jet, which took advantage of German wartime research and was the link between the first jets and the supersonic types which followed

Above: First turbojet-powered aeroplane to fly, on 27 August 1939, was the Heinkel He 178

Below: The Messerschmitt Me 262, the first German jet employed on active service during the second World War

DISCOUNTING PILOTLESS models and the German rocket-boosted glider of 1928 and 1929, the first 'jet' aircraft was one which hardly anyone today has heard. We do not even know the day on which it first flew, but Ernst Heinkel believed, from memory, after the second World War, that it was 15 June 1939. The aircraft was the He 176 rocket-plane, one of the smallest aircraft ever built and planned for an attempt on the world speed record. The He 176 was flown by Flugkapitän Erich Warsitz in the hot summer of 1939, a few weeks before he flew the somewhat larger He 178, the first aircraft ever powered by a turbojet. And on 5 April 1941 Heinkel's twin-jet fighter, the He 280, started its programme of flight trials. All three of these remarkable jet aircraft flew before any other jet in the world, except for an odd Italian machine which really was nothing more than a diversion.

In 1939 Ing Secondo Campini had managed to persuade Caproni, one of the most renowned Italian aircraft constructors, to build a prototype to test his own jet propulsion. An ordinary piston engine was used to drive a three-stage variable-pitch fan, which blew air out of a variable-area propelling nozzle at the rear of a tail-pipe in which fuel could be burned to increase thrust. The idea was sound but unsound, and the CC.2 (or N.1, as it was officially called) was a big, lumbering machine which could barely stagger off the ground when it was taken up for its first flight by Mario de Bernardi on 28 August 1940. The test authorities at Guidonia, the great Italian research establishment, did not try to conceal their ridicule; nevertheless the Caproni-Campini gained a good world press because it looked outwardly like a jet.

Despite his early lead, Ernst Heinkel was overtaken in both engines and airframes by his rivals—especially by Messerschmitt, Junkers and Arado. By far the most important German jet in the second World War was the Me 262, powered by two Jumo 004 engines—eventually rated at 1,984 lb (900 kg) thrust each—having its sweptback low wings and intended as a 525-mph (850-km/h) single-seat fighter. By the end of 1943 the first version of the Me 262 was in initial production. It carried the formidable armament of four 30-mm guns and was approximately 100 mph (160 km/h) faster than any Allied fighter it could at that time encounter. It could have won the air war for Germany single-handed. Fortunately, Hitler himself ordered its conversion into a fighter-bomber, and it was not until September 1944 that one fighter in every 13 was permitted to be used as a fighter. By the end of the war some 1,400 Me 262s had been completed, more than all other jets combined. They were formidable, but not aircraft for novices, and many inexperienced pilots were killed in Me 262 crashes in the final months of the war.

Among other significant German jets flown before 1945, two that could have proved a great thorn in the Allies' side were the Arado 234 and Heinkel 162. One was a high-wing bomber and high-altitude

reconnaissance machine, of which over 200 were built as single-seaters with two Jumo 004 engines before production switched to various bomber and fighter versions, with four BMW 003 jets and often with two seats. The He 162 'Volksjäger' was a last-ditch effort to fend off the mighty onslaught of the RAF and USAAF. A diminutive single-seat fighter, it had a high wing and twin fins between which blasted a BMW 003 turbojet mounted above the finely-streamlined fuselage.

Victorious allies can easily disregard the accomplishments of a defeated enemy, and in 1945 there was a general tendency to dismiss the incredible profusion of German jet and rocket aircraft as futuristic, impractical and merely of cursory technical interest.

This was a great mistake because, while there is no law laying down the rate of technical progress men should seek to attain, it is folly to ignore progress that is real and visible. In 1945 the German jets included prototypes with delta wings, reheat, ramjets, swept wings and even variable-geometry. Britain, in contrast, was to have nothing but conventional straight-wing fighters in service for a further ten years (apart from the American Sabre).

Yet in many ways the Allied jet technology, which for practical purposes was founded solely on the work of Sir Frank Whittle, was superior to the German. British airframe development may have seemed to range from the modest to the pathetic; and, measured against what was done under infinitely more trying conditions in Germany, British jet aircraft got off to an almost unbelievably slow start. But British jet engines were world-beaters.

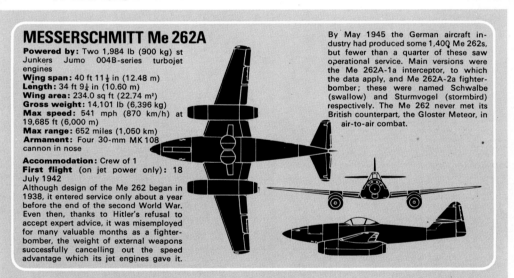

MESSERSCHMITT Me 262A

Powered by: Two 1,984 lb (900 kg) st Junkers Jumo 004B-series turbojet engines
Wing span: 40 ft 11½ in (12.48 m)
Length: 34 ft 9¼ in (10.60 m)
Wing area: 234.0 sq ft (22.74 m²)
Gross weight: 14,101 lb (6,396 kg)
Max speed: 541 mph (870 km/h) at 19,685 ft (6,000 m)
Max range: 652 miles (1,050 km)
Armament: Four 30-mm MK 108 cannon in nose

Accommodation: Crew of 1
First flight (on jet power only): 18 July 1942
Although design of the Me 262 began in 1938, it entered service only about a year before the end of the second World War. Even then, thanks to Hitler's refusal to accept expert advice, it was misemployed for many valuable months as a fighter-bomber, the weight of external weapons successfully cancelling out the speed advantage which its jet engines gave it.

By May 1945 the German aircraft industry had produced some 1,400 Me 262s, but fewer than a quarter of these saw operational service. Main versions were the Me 262A-1a interceptor, to which the data apply, and Me 262A-2a fighter-bomber; these were named Schwalbe (swallow) and Sturmvogel (stormbird) respectively. The Me 262 never met its British counterpart, the Gloster Meteor, in air-to-air combat.

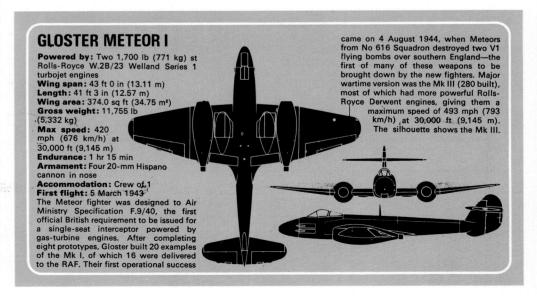

GLOSTER METEOR I

Powered by: Two 1,700 lb (771 kg) st Rolls-Royce W.2B/23 Welland Series 1 turbojet engines
Wing span: 43 ft 0 in (13.11 m)
Length: 41 ft 3 in (12.57 m)
Wing area: 374.0 sq ft (34.75 m²)
Gross weight: 11,755 lb (5,332 kg)
Max speed: 420 mph (676 km/h) at 30,000 ft (9,145 m)
Endurance: 1 hr 15 min
Armament: Four 20-mm Hispano cannon in nose
Accommodation: Crew of 1
First flight: 5 March 1943
The Meteor fighter was designed to Air Ministry Specification F.9/40, the first official British requirement to be issued for a single-seat interceptor powered by gas-turbine engines. After completing eight prototypes, Gloster built 20 examples of the Mk I, of which 16 were delivered to the RAF. Their first operational success

came on 4 August 1944, when Meteors from No 616 Squadron destroyed two V1 flying bombs over southern England—the first of many of these weapons to be brought down by the new fighters. Major wartime version was the Mk III (280 built), most of which had more powerful Rolls-Royce Derwent engines, giving them a maximum speed of 493 mph (793 km/h) at 30,000 ft (9,145 m). The silhouette shows the Mk III.

Top left: Running the engine of the Caproni-Campini N.1 with the tail section removed

Far left: Known originally as the Spider-Crab, the prototype Vampire flew in September 1943

Far left below: Prototype Gloster E.1/44 fighter of 1948, which was outdated in a sweptwing era

Left: Like the first Vampire, the prototype Lockheed XP-80 Shooting Star flew with a (D.H.) Halford H.1 turbojet

Above right: From the Shooting Star fighter was evolved the two-seat T-33A advanced trainer, which continues in service with many air forces in the early 'seventies

Right: The MiG-15 sweptwing fighter of Mikoyan and Gurevich was the first modern Soviet aircraft to challenge western leadership in the air. It was to offer tough opposition for USAF squadrons in the later war in Korea by combining German wartime sweptwing technology with the unrivalled power of Britain's Rolls-Royce Nene turbojet

It could easily have turned out differently. Pabst von Ohain ran his first engine at much the same time as did Whittle, and at that time the climate in Germany was much more favourable to the jet and other forms of aircraft gas-turbine that it was in Britain. But some essence of sheer quality in the British engineers led swiftly to better jet engines. Stanley Hooker and J P Herriot at Rolls-Royce and Major Frank B Halford and Eric S Moult at de Havilland had by 1943 created the first of a long line of British aircraft engines which have more than made up for pedestrian British aircraft and given Britain a major place in the first 30 years of the jet age.

Britain's original jet research aircraft was the Gloster E.28/39, an eminently straight-forward barrel-like machine which flew on 15 May 1941 and can today be seen in the Science Museum, London. Not including this, nor its German He 178 counterpart, while the Germans evolved 22 jet aircraft types by 1945, backed up by countless projects, Britain produced two. The Gloster Meteor and de Havilland Vampire are too well-known to call for a description, but both demonstrated qualities of tractability, safety and fitness for operational service that were less in evidence in most of the more-futuristic German machines. Both British fighters enjoyed a long period of development and a world-wide market, and a few examples of each were still in use in 1971.

In the United States jet propulsion research was very active by 1941. The Durand Committee sifted through a wide range of possible ideas and issued contracts to three firms: Westinghouse for a small axial jet, General Electric for a turboprop and Allis-Chalmers for a turbofan. In the same year Pratt & Whitney were funding their own gas-turbine research, while Lockheed, Menasco and Northrop were busy with turbojet engine and aircraft projects, and the NACA and several small firms were also active. Into this bubbling cauldron dropped the Whittle turbojet, imported from Britain at the personal urge of General 'Hap' Arnold, Chief of Staff of the Army Air Force. General Electric swiftly 'Americanised' the Whittle unit and ran its own engine after only 28 weeks, in March 1942. Two of these engines took the first Bell XP-59A Airacomet into the air on 1 October that year, but the P-59 was hardly an advance on the piston-engined Mustang. Lockheed, however, teamed up with de Havilland's Goblin engine—the turbojet used in the Vampire—and created the XP-80 Shooting Star. This was a world-beater, a trim, flashing fighter which could outmanoeuvre and in most respects outperform every other aircraft in the world when it flew in January 1944. Powered in its production form by the more powerful General Electric I-40 (later called the Allison J33), the F-80 bore the brunt of early combat in Korea and still serves in two-seat training form as the T-33A. It was followed by the F-84 Thunderjet and the remarkable swept-wing F-86 Sabre, and it was the Sabre that led the way to the supersonic fighters of today.

In the Soviet Union a great deal of work had been done on rocket-powered aircraft, and a possible prototype of a rocket fighter was flown in 1942; but turbojet development had to wait for German and British technology to become available in 1945. The BMW, Junkers and Heinkel-Hirth engines were all studied carefully and the first two were actually used in hasty but successful conversions of existing piston-engined fighters. But Soviet fighter design was suddenly put on the map by the MiG-15, first flown in the summer of 1947 with a Rolls-Royce Nene which the British government shipped at just the right time. Klimov soon had similar and improved versions of the Nene in massive production, making possible the production versions of both the MiG-15 and the Il-28 bomber.

Many other nations were eager to share in the new form of propulsion. In Japan a simple, underpowered twin-engined jet fighter just managed to log 11 minutes in the air in the final days of the war. In France a jet research aircraft, together with various jet and turboprop engines, was schemed during the German occupation, and the SO.6000 Triton flew with a Jumo 004 in November 1946. The Swedes found to their delight that the excellent British Goblin turbojet fitted like a glove into the engine bay of the twin-boom pusher J 21 fighter, and lost no time in installing one of these engines in place of the original Daimler-Benz DB 605 piston-engine. The resulting J 21R began its very successful career in March 1947. Five months later a jet fighter designed and built wholly in Argentina began its flight trials: the Pulqui (Arrow), powered by a Rolls-Royce Derwent.

Jet propulsion rapidly became international. It was only natural that all the first jets should have been fighters. Today most nations are more concerned with air transport. It is no exaggeration to claim that it was the jet, especially in the form of the turbofan, that turned air transport into the efficient giant it is today.

The First 'Post-War' Wars

Top: Korea marked the operational swan-song of the F-51 Mustang in USAF service. In a jet age it gave fine service as a ground-attack aircraft

Centre, left to right:
While marking targets for attack in Korea, Harvards often attracted considerable ground fire, but even this one got home safely

As a change from 'ghost' attacks on terrorists in the jungle, men of the RAAF's No 1 Squadron take some of their gallant Gurkha allies for a 'flip' in a Lincoln bomber

Meteor F.8 jet-fighters of No 77 Squadron, RAAF, which gave good service alongside the USAF in Korea, although outclassed by Chinese MiG-15s

Right: The helicopter was, perhaps, the greatest discovery of the Korean War. This Marine Sikorsky H05S (S-52), evacuating wounded from a front-line area, was able to carry the men straight to base hospital in relative comfort, over almost impossible terrain. The percentage of casualties who died was the lowest in military history thanks to the 'choppers'

Above: As well as evacuating casualties, helicopters like this Sikorsky HRS (S-55) ferried ammunition and supplies to hilltop positions that no other vehicle could have reached

Top right: One of the strangest aspects of the Korean War was that combat aircraft of both sides often took off from bases in countries that were never subjected to enemy attack. It was quite safe for Captain Johnnie Gosnell's family to wave him farewell as he took off from Japan in his Twin Mustang for a sortie over the war zone

Right: F-80 Shooting Stars of the USAF's 51st Fighter Interceptor Wing used JATO rockets to help them lift heavy loads from short Korean runways

THE OLD ADAGE that necessity is the mother of invention is never more true than in wartime. In the two great wars since aviation began, the pace of military aircraft development was dramatically increased over that which has occurred in time of comparative peace.

But one must stress the 'comparative', for since the end of the second World War there has ___ r been, for the major powers, real peace. While the strategic nuclear balance—the balance of terror—has involved the two 'super-powers' in rapid development of aircraft, missiles and other weaponry, there has been a rash of confined 'brushfire' wars and counter-insurgency campaigns which have also affected aircraft development.

The profusion of these wars until about the mid-1960s was one outcome of the balance of terror. Locked as they were in a nuclear stalemate, with Armageddon as the inevitable outcome of open conflict, the two big power blocs grappled and probed each other's weaknesses, each seeking an advantage, often on the territory of the uncommitted nations of the 'third world', or of puppet states and colonial territories.

First and biggest of these wars was that which began in 1950 in partitioned Korea. A Chinese-inspired Communist North Korea invaded and largely overran the US-supported South Korea. Many nations sent forces to fight under the United Nations banner—in fact this Korean campaign is the largest conflict to have involved the UN collectively—while opposing Chinese forces entered the fray on a massive scale.

Effectively, only the United States forces and the RAAF fought for the south in the Korean air war, with RAF Sunderlands flying maritime reconnaissance against seaborne incursions and movement around the Korean peninsula.

For the US forces, it was the first com-

mitment in combat of jet aircraft, though that magnificent piston-engined fighter of the second World War, the F-51 Mustang, was heavily engaged as a ground-attack aircraft. Following the overt entry of Communist China into the war, many were the dog-fights in the skies above North Korea which engaged, principally, China's Soviet-supplied MiG-15s and the USAF's F-86 Sabres, together with carrier-borne USN jet fighters operating from flat-tops in the South China Sea.

Technically, the MiG-15 and the F-86 were closely matched, though the superior training and tactics of the US pilots gave them a clear margin in combat—still, at that time, fought with guns rather than air-to-air missiles. But this was hardly surprising—Communist China as an undivided mainland state was only two years old when the war began and the massive build-up of her air forces, even with Russian advisers, resulted in tyro pilots meeting in combat experienced veterans of the second World War.

US President Harry S Truman forbade his forces (the UN contingents were effectively under US command) from taking the war beyond the Yalu River, the border between North Korea and Communist China, and even aerial hot pursuit was forbidden. The Chinese airmen, therefore, had a safe sanctuary in operating from Chinese bases and they confined their incursions only to a relatively narrow band of North Korean airspace beyond the river. Elsewhere, Allied supremacy in the air was total.

The RAAF's unit was 77 Squadron, sent originally in the air fighting role with Meteor F.8s but found to be outclassed in combat by the more manoeuvrable MiG-15, even when flown by less experienced pilots. The unit was therefore switched to ground attack, in which it fought alongside USAF

units equipped primarily with the F-84C Thunderjet and USN Skyraiders from carriers offshore. Light bombers ___ ing from the second World W__ ___arly the Douglas Invader, we__ ___ heavily engaged.

Korea saw the first use of that horrifying air-dropped weapon, napalm ___ ___ technically, the war's main outcome w__ the rapid development of helicopter ___ methods of their deployment. Whe__ the war began helicopters were still none-too-numerous military novelties; ___ __ cease-fire in 1953 they were standard ___ols of military forces with a vast accumulation of operational experience behind them.

It was in casualty evacuation and combat rescue that they were most use__ The feat of the combat rescue helicopter ___ par ticular, drew the world' ___ admiration Frequently making lo__ __rsions into enemy-held territory under aerial top-cover they rescued downed pilots from beneath 'rescue caps' of ground-strafing aircraft which kept enemy forces away from the men being rescued. The te__niqu__ ate became standard in Vietnam ___ and if Korea has a place in aviation histor__ __t is for it demonstration of the military potential of the helicopter.

Concurrently with Korea, British Commonwealth forces were engaged in their own lower-key, immensely-drawn-out brushfire war against Communist guerillas operating in the dense jungle country of Malaya. This campaign lasted more than 10 years and was always one of ___ unching at shadows; eventually it was ___ by the success of the 'hearts and minds' campaign in which the guerillas were denied the support and succour of the local populace and, quite literally, starved into defeat.

But it was a war in which air power was used to a limited extent, for reconnaissance and for blasting hard-to-find terrorist jungle hide-outs. Principally, piston-engined aircraft of second World War vintage were used by RAF making a big contribution with their own bombers and the main RAF types during the earlier years being Mosquitos, Hornets and Brigands. Ultimately a technique was evolved under which well-developed ground intelligence networks, native trackers and radio monitoring were used to track Communist movements, after which air strikes were called in. The successful conclusion of the campaign was followed only a few years later by the opening of another Malaysian chapter, confrontation with Indonesia, whose regime objected to the creation of the Malaysian Federation. In this three-year war the same techniques, and many more helicopters, were used.

Throughout the 'fifties there were numerous conflicts involving other colonial territories. While decolonisation of many French territories went smoothly, very bitter and complex guerilla wars were fought in Indochina (where the conflict was no more than a prelude to the later Vietnam war and was merely one phase in 30 years of continuous warfare there) and in Algeria. The French made heavy use of paratroops in both theatres, but their air support was always less than adequate.

Helicopters were employed more heavily with the passing of the years and were soon seen, as in other brushfire wars, to be extremely vulnerable to small-arms sharp-shooting from the ground, a problem which eventually leads to a high rate of attrition in hot-war operations. France fought these wars with a miscellany of equipment, much of it retired from the second World War, and the Algerian conflict will be remembered as the last operational use for the 'Jug'— the great fighter-bomber, the F-47 Thunderbolt.

In Kenya in the early 'fifties Britain was faced with an infinitely bizarre war, if one can call it that—the Mau-Mau campaign. This was more the uprising of a particular tribal faction, an emergency of blood-chilling but comparatively small-scale atrocities. Again, the air power task was to hit jungle hide-outs and keep terrorists on the move by air strikes against their lairs with an ad hoc collection of equipment. Lincolns were used, as were armed Harvard

This page, top to bottom:
Noratlas transport aircraft of the French Air Force were used very effectively to drop parachute troops during the brief Suez campaign of 1956

The 'invasion' stripes around the rear fuselage of these French Mystere IV-A fighters identify them as aircraft deployed for use at Suez

This Hunter F.Mk 5 of No 34 Squadron was one of the newest types equipping the 34 RAF Squadrons based in Malta and Cyprus for action during the Suez fighting

French counterpart of the Hunter was this F-84F Thunderstreak of the 3e Escadre, photographed at Akrotiri, Cyprus

Piston-engined aircraft like this rocket-armed Brigand were ideal for the wearisome job of trying to track down and attack terrorists in the jungles of Malaya

BRISTOL BRIGAND

Powered by: Two 2,470 hp (2,810 hp with methanol/water injection) Bristol Centaurus 57 eighteen-cylinder radial engines, each driving a 14 ft 0 in (4.27 m) diameter four-blade propeller
Wing span: 72 ft 4 in (22.05 m)
Length: 46 ft 5 in (14.15 m)
Wing area: 718 sq ft (66.70 m²)
Gross weight: 39,000 lb (17,690 kg)
Max speed: 358 mph (576 km/h) at 16,000 ft (4,880 m)
Max range: 2,800 miles (4,506 km)
Accommodation: Crew of 3
Armament: Four 20-mm cannon in underside of nose; bombs or mine under

the fuselage, and one bomb or four rocket projectiles beneath each wing
First flight: 4 December 1944
Progressive development of the wartime Beaufighter yielded a small family of twin-engined, twin-tailed Bristol designs: the Buckingham, Buckmaster and Brigand. The Brigand was originally designated as a torpedo-carrying fighter, but in practice was used mainly as a light bomber and ground attack aircraft. It came into its own during the anti-terrorist campaigns in Malaya during 1950-54, when it was operated with considerable success by Nos 45 and 84 Squadrons of the RAF.

trainers, and in this campaign much valuable work was performed by reservist fliers and light aircraft pilots.

The 'brushfire' era saw, in 1956, a week-long 'war' quite unlike any of the others. This was the Anglo-French invasion of the Suez Canal Zone, in company with Israel, following the Egyptian government's decision to nationalise the Suez Canal. The seaborne assault was in the classic second World War pattern, with a substantial invasion fleet assembled off Port Said. Air strikes against Canal Zone air bases were flown by both British and French fighter-bombers from carriers and from bases in Cyprus, while longer-range attacks on targets around Cairo were mounted from Malta by Canberras and Valiants, the latter then newly in service and operating not in their nuclear design role but with the high-altitude high-explosive precision-bombing techniques of the second World War.

But though classical in concept, the operation was not a classic in execution. It was badly bungled and it ended on a note of political farce when strong United Nations disapproval and in particular the outspoken condemnation of the United States caused the Anglo-French forces to withdraw before advancing along the full length of the Canal. Meteors, Venoms and Vampires were the strike aircraft used by the RAF, while Fleet Air Arm Wyverns and Sea Venoms also took part. Again, the only significant feature of the Suez operation, so far as aviation history is concerned, was the use made of helicopters in the assault landing, in which to a large extent they replaced the highly-vulnerable inshore landing craft used in similar assaults during the second World War.

By 1956 neither the French nor the British forces were well enough endowed with helicopters able to lift significant pay-loads (the biggest in British service were Westland S-55s), and the small number assembled were drawn from naval anti-submarine units and a joint RAF/Army experimental helicopter trials unit. They performed well—against virtually no opposition—and set a pattern from which helicopter tactical assault squadrons, and the Royal Navy's commando carriers, evolved naturally.

Above: Five squadrons of Royal Navy Sea Venoms from the carriers *Albion* **and** *Eagle* **flew side-by-side with four RAF Venom squadrons from Cyprus in devastating ground-attack operations which helped to eliminate the Egyptian Air Force. Most of the 120 MiGs and 50 Il-28 jet bombers that had been supplied by Russia were wiped out on the ground; only eight were lost in air combat over Suez**

Right: Skyraider attack aircraft of the US Navy first displayed their great versatility and hitting power in Korea. But they were to add immeasurably to their 'battle honours' in a later, even tougher war in Vietnam

BROKEN BARRIERS

Opposite page, top: First aeroplane to exceed the speed of sound was the Bell X-1. Later versions of the same design were the X-1A and X-1B, shown here. Although comparatively simple and straight-winged. the X-1A had logged a speed of no less than Mach 2.42 by June 1954

Bottom: Most US high-speed research aircraft have been designed for air-launching from 'mother-planes', to conserve their rocket propellants for brief dashes at maximum speed. This photograph shows the swept-wing Bell X-2 cradled under the cutaway bomb-bay of a B-50 Superfortress

Above: The X-1B in flight, after release from its B-29 'mother-plane'. This aircraft was specially equipped to investigate the thermal problems of high-speed flying

Below: Starting the rocket engine of the X-2 after release from a B-50. As always, an F-86 'chase-plane' is in attendance, its pilot watching closely to check that all is well and ready to offer help in an emergency. On more than one occasion 'chase' pilots have guided other aircraft to a safe landing when their pilots have run into difficulties

Bottom: The swept-wing X-2 did not enjoy the success of the X-1 family, both examples being destroyed in accidents. On its fatal last flight, one of them reached a speed of Mach 3.2, setting a record which was unbeaten for five years

FOR RESIDENTS IN the Worthing and Portsmouth areas of England's South Coast, Saturday 10 March 1956 was unusually noisy. What the London evening newspapers described as 'particularly heavy' sonic booms on that day disturbed residents enjoying the early Spring sunshine. Sonic booms were a manifestation of a flying phenomenon which had received wide publicity in the years following the second World War—the phenomenon of the 'sound barrier'. However, not only the sound barrier was being broken on that sunny March day; the '1,000 mph' barrier was also being broken as the Fairey Delta 2 research aircraft outpaced the sun to set a four-figure (in mph) World Air Speed Record for the first time.

Both of these 'barriers' exist more in the minds of journalists than in fact. No physical barriers exist to impede the passage of aeroplanes through the air, and today supersonic flight—ie, flight at speeds greater than the speed of sound, or beyond the 'sound barrier'—is a commonplace, experienced not only by highly-trained professionals but by passengers in the new generation of supersonic transports like the Concorde. For a time, it is true, the 'sound barrier' did seem to represent a hazard, causing aircraft to behave strangely as their speed approached that of sound. [The speed of sound is usually referred to as Mach 1, and it varies from about 760 mph (1,223 km/h) at sea level to 660 mph (1,062 km/h) at 36,000 ft (11,000 m), above which height it remains constant. In the same way, Mach 2 means twice the speed of sound at any given altitude, and so on.]

At Mach 1, the behaviour of the airflow around an aircraft changes, giving rise to a shock wave and other effects which could cause control of the aircraft to be lost, or could create such a high drag that Mach 1 could not actually be surpassed at all. Once these phenomena were fully understood, it became relatively simple to design aeroplanes in such a way that the so-called 'barrier' could be surmounted smoothly, with virtually no effects noticeable within the aircraft.

The possibility that some kind of barrier to high-speed flight might exist was first realised during the second World War, when the effects of compressibility (that is, the air becoming compressed ahead of a fast-travelling aeroplane) were first experienced with such aeroplanes as the Supermarine Spitfire and Lockheed Lightning. In a maximum power dive, the Spitfire could reach speeds equivalent to about 9/10ths the speed of sound—fast enough for compressibility to be experienced. At about the same time, it became clear that the advent of the jet engine would make even higher speeds possible, and serious research into the so-called sound barrier began.

Credit for the design of Britain's first supersonic aeroplane goes to the Miles company, which was officially commissioned in 1943 to design and produce a jet-plane capable of flying at 1,000 mph (1,609 km/h) at 36,000 ft (11,000 m)—more than double the speed of the fastest aeroplane then in service. The Miles design, known as the M.52, was well advanced by 1946, when the whole programme was officially cancelled on the flimsy pretext that manned flight at such a speed was too dangerous. No such trivial excuses were allowed to stand in the way of the parallel American research programme which, started a year after the M.52, led to the construction of the world's first supersonic aeroplane, the Bell X-1.

The design of the X-1, which was conceived originally to fly at only a little above the speed of sound, was similar in many general respects to that of the M.52. It had a very thin-section wing, without any sweepback, but a major difference was that the X-1 was rocket-powered, and therefore had to be air-launched after being carried aloft beneath the fuselage of a B-29 Superfortress. The first air-launch of the X-1 was made on 19 January 1946, but powered flights were not attempted until 9 December of that year, using the second prototype. Nearly another year passed before supersonic flight was achieved, this milestone being reached by Captain Charles 'Chuck' Yeager on 14 October 1947.

The speed reached by the X-1 on that historic occasion was 670 mph (1,078 km/h) at a height of 42,000 ft (12,800 m), and therefore equivalent to a Mach number of 1.015. In all, six members of the X-1 'family' were built; in one of them, the X-1A, Yeager reached a speed of Mach 2.42 on 4 June 1954. This achievement emphasised that, whatever impediment might have existed to flight at Mach 1, once that point had been surpassed no further aerodynamic 'barrier' remained. An aeroplane designed to overcome compressibility effects at the speed of sound could be accelerated beyond Mach 1 to the limits imposed by the available engine thrust or until a much more cogent barrier was encountered—the 'heat barrier'.

Heat becomes a problem at very high speeds because of the friction between the surface of the aeroplane and the molecules of air in contact with it. This friction causes the skin, and therefore the inside of the aeroplane, to heat up; and for flight at speeds much above Mach 2 special precautions have to be taken. The temperatures that can be reached not only degrade the strength of the metal structure but can also cause such unpleasant effects as boiling in the fuel tanks.

For the next research step beyond the X-1, therefore, Bell elected to use a stainless steel airframe, together with sweptback wings. The resultant X-2 appeared in 1952, but the two prototypes of this design were dogged by misfortune, both being destroyed in accidents. Before the second X-2 crashed in 1956, however, it reached a speed of Mach 3.2 (2,094 mph; 3,370 km/h), and this remained the highest speed at which man had flown until 1961.

The X-2, it will be noted, exceeded Mach 3 only a few months after the Fairey Delta 2 set the first 'over 1,000 mph' speed record. As the X-1 and X-2 were air-launched, they could not set records under the terms laid

down by the FAI, but ever since 1946 the USA has had a clear lead over other nations in 'barrier-breaking' research aeroplanes. The first British aeroplane capable of bettering Mach 1 in level flight was the English Electric P.1A, which first exceeded the speed of sound on 11 August 1954 and provided the basis for the RAF's first truly supersonic fighter, the Lightning. The first British supersonic flight (in a dive) had been made on 9 September 1948 by John Derry in the D.H.108.

In France, supersonic flight research began somewhat later than in Britain, the first aeroplane capable of exceeding Mach 1 being the Sud-Ouest S.O. 9000 Trident, first flown on 2 March 1953. Straight-winged like the Bell X-1, the Trident had two turbojet engines and a rocket unit to boost it to a maximum speed of Mach 1.6. French experience of supersonic flight was then extended by the delta-winged SFECMAS Gerfaut which, on 3 August 1954, became the first aeroplane in Europe to exceed Mach 1 in level flight on the power of a turbojet alone, without rocket or afterburner. Further development of the design by Nord led to the Nord 1500 Griffon, which was powered by a ramjet and achieved Mach 1.85 in 1957.

Whilst the work in France and Britain provided a basis for the design of operational aircraft with supersonic performance, following the American lead, a further research programme was put in hand in the USA which led to production of the most remarkable research aeroplane flown to date. This programme evolved from discussions that started in mid-1954, between representatives of the USAF, USN and NACA, with the aim of defining new objectives for flight research beyond the X-1 and X-2. By the end of the year, it was agreed that the objective would be an aeroplane capable of flying at 4,500 mph (7,240 km/h; nearly Mach 7) and reaching an altitude of 250,000 ft (76,200 m). The primary structure would be required to withstand temperatures as high as 1,200°F, with heating rates of 30 BTU per sq ft of surface area per second.

In every respect, the requirement was far ahead of the state of the art in 1955, but the programme went ahead rapidly and with remarkably few setbacks, considering its radical nature. North American Aviation won the design contest and was awarded a development contract on 30 September 1955. The aircraft was designated X-15 and was designed around an XLR99 liquid-fuel rocket engine capable of delivering a thrust of more than 60,000 lb (27,215 kg) for a period of several minutes. Like the X-1, the X-15 was to be air-launched, since precious fuel could not be expended in getting the X-15 off the ground and up to operating altitudes. Two Boeing B-52s were therefore modified as carriers for the X-15s, three of which were ordered. With a span of only 22 ft (6.70 m) for the slightly swept-back trapezoidal wings (again reminiscent of the Miles M.52 design) the X-15 had a gross weight at launch of over 31,000 lb (14,060 kg), of which more than 18,000 lb (8,165 kg) was accounted for by the liquid

Opposite page: The North American X-15 rocket-powered research aircraft in its original form. Before it completed its test programme, this remarkable aeroplane attained a speed of 4,534 mph (7,297 km/h)— the fastest man has yet travelled in anything but a spacecraft

This page, top to bottom:
The X-15 was fitted with a conventional nose-wheel unit. In this picture the tail is supported on a ground trolley. The aircraft landed on two retractable steel tail-skids

The stubby Fairey F.D.1 research aircraft spanned a mere 19 ft 6½ in (5.95 m), which gave it a fantastic rate of roll

The French SFECMAS Gerfaut was the first aeroplane in Europe to exceed Mach 1 on the power of a turbojet engine alone in level flight, on 3 August 1954

Even more spectacular was the Nord Griffon, the whole body of which formed the outer casing of a huge ramjet engine. A turbojet mounted in the centre of the ramjet provided power for take-off and low-speed flying, and a means of igniting the ramjet itself

oxygen and anhydrous ammonia rocket propellants.

When the first X-15 free flight was made on 8 June 1959 the aircraft was fitted with lower-powered engines, as the XLR99 was not then ready. With two XLR11-RM-5s, giving a combined thrust of about 33,000 lb (15,000 kg), the first powered flight was made by the second X-15 prototype on 17 September 1959, a speed of Mach 2.3 being achieved. From that point on, both the speed and the altitude reached by the X-15s climbed steadily, with Mach 3 being reached in November 1961 after the XLR99 engine had been fitted in the second prototype. By December 1963 the X-15s had reached a speed of Mach 6.06, had encountered a skin temperature of 1,320°F and reached an altitude of 314,750 ft (95,936 m).

Following a landing accident with the No 2 X-15 in 1962, this aircraft was rebuilt as the X-15A-2, with a number of modifications to permit an even higher performance, and first flew in this guise on 28 June 1964. In October 1967, this X-15 reached a speed of 4,534 mph (7,297 km/h), equivalent to Mach 6.72 and matching the original design requirement. This is the highest recorded speed yet achieved by man in an aeroplane capable of being controlled in normal flight.

Higher speeds than those mentioned above have been experienced by astronauts in space capsules orbiting the Earth or in a lunar trajectory. Whether there is any practical use for such speeds in travelling between two points on the Earth's surface remains to be proved. Limits there certainly are, so far as everyday travel is concerned; but they are limits imposed by the habits and requirements of the traveller rather than by any physical limitations on the aeroplane. The barriers, such as they were, have been broken and the high speed research conducted during the past 25 years has provided all the information needed to design and build the fastest aeroplanes likely to be required for military or commercial purposes for many decades to come. When the destination is the stars, other unknown barriers may still await discovery—but that is another story, another day.

MILES M.52

Powered by: One Power Jets W.2/700 turbojet engine, delivering 2,000 lb (907 kg) st at S/L and fitted with augmentor and afterburning planned to give 4,100 lb (1,860 kg) st at max design speed
Wing span: 27 ft 0 in (8.23 m)
Length: 28 ft 7 in (8.71 m)
Wing area: 143 sq ft (13.28 m²)
Design gross weight: 7,710 lb (3,497 kg)
Max design speed: 1,000 mph (1,609 km/h) at 36,000 ft (11,000 m) after a dive from 50,000 ft (15,240 m)
Accommodation: Crew of 1
First flight: intended for 1946
Designed to meet Specification E.24/43, which called for an aeroplane capable of flying more than twice as fast as any that had previously flown in level flight, the Miles M.52 could have been the world's

first supersonic aircraft, only a year after the end of the second World War. Its ultra-thin, bi-convex wings had been flight tested on the Miles 'Gillette Falcon', and it had other advanced features such as an annular air intake, all-moving tailplane, and a complete escape capsule for the pilot. Three prototypes were ordered, and the first of these was half-completed when the project was cancelled by the British government in February 1946. The design was later fully vindicated by the success of test models built and flown by Vickers in 1947-48—but not until 1956 did a British jet aircraft (the Fairey Delta 2) reach the speed expected of the M.52.

DE HAVILLAND D.H.108

Powered by: One 3,750 lb (1,701 kg) st de Havilland Goblin 4 turbojet
Wing span: 39 ft 0 in (11.89 m)
Length: 26 ft 9½ in (8.17 m)
Wing area: 328 sq ft (30.47 m²)
Max level speed: approx 560 mph (900 km/h) at 45,000 ft (13,720 m) (Mach 0.85)
Max attained speed: Mach 1 in a dive between 40,000 ft (12,200 m) and 30,000 ft (9,145 m)
Accommodation: Crew of 1
First flight: 15 May 1946 (first prototype)
Designed to Specification E.18/45, to provide flight experience of the tailless configuration planned for de Havilland's D.H.106 airliner (which eventually emerged

as the Comet), the D.H.108 was among the first aircraft to suffer, dramatically, from the effects of compressibility on an airframe in the transonic speed range. Originally, two prototypes were built, one each for low-speed and high-speed flight, and in the second of these Geoffrey de Havilland lost his life when the aeroplane broke up over the Thames Estuary in September 1946. A third prototype was built as a replacement, with several design improvements. In 1948 it set up a new 100-km closed-circuit speed record of 605.23 mph (974 km/h) and on 9 September 1948 became the first British aircraft (and the world's first jet aircraft) to exceed Mach 1. Data apply to this third prototype.

Opposite page, top: The Fairey Delta 2, first aeroplane to set up an 'over-1,000 mph' speed record, in 1956. It also pioneered the type of drooping nose now fitted to the Concorde and Tu-144 supersonic airliners

Bottom: First flown on 16 May 1957, the Saunders-Roe S-R.53 was an experimental 'mixed-power' interceptor, powered by a Viper turbojet and a de Havilland Spectre variable-thrust rocket engine for rapid climb and combat boost. It was intended to be armed with two wingtip-mounted Firestreak missiles. Its production development, the P.177, was cancelled under one of a series of government economy measures

This page, top: Another mixed-power experimental fighter design was the French S.O.9000 Trident, which pioneered supersonic flight research in France

Centre: This rear view of the Trident shows well the three chambers of its SEPR 25 rocket engine, in the tail, and the wingtip-mounted turbojets. The designed top speed was Mach 1.6 for a duration of $4\frac{1}{2}$ minutes

Bottom: End product of years of supersonic research in Britain was the superb Lightning interceptor. In this view, the Lightning has underwing bombs and two overwing jettisonable auxiliary fuel tanks for ferrying

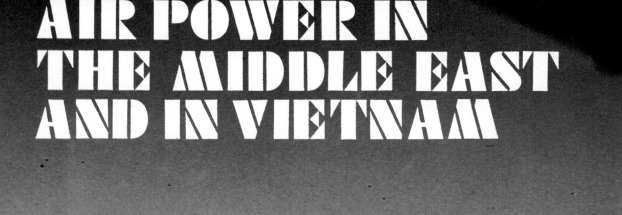

AIR POWER IN THE MIDDLE EAST AND IN VIETNAM

The so-called periods 'between the wars' and 'after the war' have in fact hardly ever been free of national or international conflict somewhere in the world, often resulting in changes in concepts of aerial warfare. In Vietnam, where conditions did not favour use of complex supersonic aircraft, Vought's subsonic A-7 Corsair II proved highly effective as an attack aircraft, and the jungle terrain necessitated a widespread return to the camouflage techniques of earlier days

SINCE THE MID-1960s there have been two wars quite unlike any others in history, and both have had profound effects on the development of military aviation, on technology and on strategies.

One, the June 1967 clash between Israel and neighbouring Arab states, lasted six days. The other, in Vietnam, began in earnest in 1965, and is merely the latest phase in almost 30 years of continuous warfare in the area.

The 'six-day war' was one of history's shortest and most brilliant against-the-odds campaigns. It was a conflict won entirely by the inspired use of airpower, and is the outstanding example of the pre-emptive strike—hitting the enemy so hard, so early, before he is able to bring into play his numerically superior forces, that victory is almost inevitable.

It began shortly after dawn on 5 June. In flights of four, Israeli fighter-bombers swept in very low over the Sinai desert and the Nile delta. They attacked 19 Egyptian air bases—one flight to each airfield. Lined up in serried ranks, and sometimes in revetments, was Egypt's massive Soviet-supplied air fleet—more than a hundred MiG-21s, squadrons of Tu-16 and Il-28 bombers, MiG-17, MiG-19 and Su-7 strike fighters, and hosts of transports and helicopters.

On their first strike, the Israelis ignored all these. Flying low, avoiding radar detection, catching the Egyptian anti-aircraft defences unawares and below the altitudes at which their SAM 2 missiles could be used, they flew straight down the runways after pulling up to a height of about 300 ft (90 m).

They were flying fast—about 575 mph (927 km/h)—and they dropped an entirely new type of bomb. It had to be new, for any conventional bomb dropped at this combination of speed and height would bounce and skitter to the horizon, if it did not explode on first impact and destroy the aircraft that dropped it.

These bombs were different. Developed in Israel, they had four powerful retro-rockets to slow them after separation from the aircraft. After a fraction of a second a drogue mounted in the tail deployed, slowing them further. The drag also rotated the bomb nose downwards. After an angle of 60°-80° to the horizontal was reached, four booster rockets ignited to blast the bomb downwards, into the runway, without bounce. By this time the aircraft that dropped it was safely—about four seconds—away. And then it exploded, with quite a modest bang, blowing a crater in the runway.

Two or three such craters, neatly stitched along or across a runway, rendered it useless. The Egyptian Air Force was grounded and, when the second and third waves of Israeli aircraft came in, its aircraft were sitting-duck targets for conventional rocket and cannon strafing. Literally in their hundreds they went up in flames, their columns of smoke appearing as funeral pyres against the desert sky.

Later in the day it was the turn of the Jordanian and Syrian air forces to receive

Above, top to bottom: The element of surprise, and the pin-point accuracy with which its 'concrete dibber' bombs were dropped on Egyptian runways, enabled the Israeli Air Force to achieve almost complete sovereignty of the air on the first day of the 'six-day war'. From then onwards Arab aircraft, like this burnt-out Egyptian MiG-17, were sitting-duck targets for later air strikes

Used to increasing advantage in Vietnam, the FAC (forward air control) aircraft acted as a pathfinder to mark strike targets and could also loiter long enough to observe the results. Aircraft like this O-2A, military counterpart of the Cessna Super Skymaster, can carry rocket pods and other ordnance to conduct light strikes of their own if necessary

Part of the US policy in South Vietnam was to build up the strength of the country's own air force—providing yet another livery for the ubiquitous Douglas C-47 to wear

Opposite page, top: Specially developed to the particular needs of the war in Vietnam, the Bell AH-1G HueyCobra was the first of the new class of helicopter 'gunships', combining a 219 mph (352 km/h) top speed with a powerful armament and a fuselage only about 4 ft (1.22 m) wide which makes it difficult for enemy gunners to hit

Centre: Part of the assembly line at Fort Worth, Texas, which up to mid-1974 had received orders for more than 1,100 HueyCobras for the US forces. The extremely slim profile is particularly evident from this angle

Bottom: One of the least cost-effective aspects of the war in Vietnam was the carpet-bombing of relatively small areas of jungle using huge B-52 Stratofortresses. Flying these eight-engined, global-range giants more than 5,000 miles (8,050 km) to a target, often to little or no effect, savoured of using the proverbial steam-hammer to crack a nut

the same treatment. Then, on the Tuesday, the nearer Iraqi bases got it. In one hammer blow, the IAF had established total air command which enabled the Israeli ground forces to achieve all their objectives—to reach the Suez Canal, conquer the Syrian Golan Heights, thrust south to Sharm el Sheik, push the Jordanians east of the River Jordan, and seize the old city of Jerusalem—all by 6 pm on Saturday, when a cease-fire was declared. The war was over, though the insoluble political situation is with us still.

The Israelis had appreciated and exploited the greatest weakness of modern jet warplanes, with their high-pressure tyres, their long field distances (lengthened still more by reduced power in high desert temperatures) and their engines' inability to withstand the ingestion of stones. The aircraft were unable to take off from the hot, sharp gravel of the Sinai, or soft delta soil, without 8,000-10,000 ft (2,440-3,050 m) of ribbon-smooth concrete beneath them. Without it they were useless—and without it, they were destroyed.

All else that followed was mere detail against this one essential strike. As an example of the Israelis' precise planning, and the accuracy of their bombing, some Egyptian runways in Sinai were bombed to a specific length. Though the strikes grounded the resident MiGs, sufficient length was left undamaged to accept Israeli transports a few days later when the bases were over-run—a requirement which was met by putting two or three craters across a jet runway about one-third of the way along it.

Other aspects of the Israelis' air war would be farcical had they not been effective. Armed Magister trainers, flown by reservists, were used in the heavy fighting for East Jerusalem. And not only by day, for by night a massive searchlight set up on a tall trade union building in the Israeli part of the city served to illuminate the adjacent Jordanian slopes for the merciless onslaught to continue.

Great confusion was caused among the airborne remnants of the Arab air forces by Arabic-speaking Israelis broadcasting on their frequencies, giving false orders, countermanding others—an extension of an RAF Bomber Command technique used over Germany in the second World War, when RAF bombers carried native German speakers for the same purpose.

As for improvisation—if you have no anti-submarine aircraft then a rear-loading transport, like the Noratlas, makes a good alternative. Load up with depth charges, fly with the rear doors open and then, if one of your naval craft radios you a suspected contact, slip the lashings, push the throttles forward, pull up the nose and over the sill they roll. . . .

*　　*　　*

For the Americans there was to be not six days but well over six years of frustrating agony following their unequivocal entry into Vietnam in 1965, after nine years' involvement as numerically limited and ostensibly non-combatant 'advisers'.

For 2½ years they hammered away in a

REPUBLIC F-105 THUNDERCHIEF

Powered by: One 26,500 lb (12,030 kg) st Pratt & Whitney J75-P-19W afterburning turbojet engine
Wing span: 34 ft 11¼ in (10.65 m)
Length: 67 ft 0¼ in (20.43 m)
Wing area: 385 sq ft (35.77 m²)
Gross weight: 52,545 lb (23,814 kg)
Max speed: 1,485 mph (2,390 km/h) at 36,000 ft (11,000 m)
Typical combat radius: 920 miles (1,480 km)
Armament: One 20-mm General Electric Vulcan multi-barrel cannon in fuselage; more than 14,000 lb (6,350 kg) of bombs, rockets, napalm containers or drop-tanks under wings and fuselage.

Accommodation: Crew of 1
First flights: 22 October 1955 (YF-105); 9 June 1959 (F-105D)
One of the most sophisticated aircraft to be thrown into the struggle in Vietnam, the Thunderchief has been called by publicists a 'one-man air force'; to its crews it is known affectionately as the 'Thud'. Major version is the all-weather F-105D (data and silhouette), which entered USAF service in 1960; more than 600 of this model were built. In August 1969 the first example was flown of a modified F-105D, distinguishable by its 'saddleback' dorsal fairing which contains the electronics for a new T-Stick II integral bombing system; about 30 other Thunderchiefs were similarly modernised in 1970.

BELL AH-1 HUEYCOBRA

Powered by: One 1,400 shp Lycoming T53-L-13 turboshaft engine, derated to 1,100 shp
Main rotor diameter: 44 ft 0 in (13.41 m)
Fuselage length: 44 ft 5 in (13.54 m)
Main rotor disc area: 1,520.4 sq ft (141.2 m²)
Gross weight: 9,500 lb (4,309 kg)
Max speed: 219 mph (352 km/h)
Max range: 387 miles (622 km)
Armament: XM-28 'chin' turret, mounting either two 7.62-mm six-barrel Miniguns, two 40-mm grenade launchers, or one Minigun and one grenade launcher; racks under stub-wings for four rocket packs, two Minigun pods or two TOW missile pods

Accommodation: Crew of 2
First flight: 7 September 1965
Developed privately by Bell as a small, agile, well-armed 'gunship' helicopter, the HueyCobra was adopted by the US Army in 1966 and entered service in Vietnam in mid-1967 as the AH-1G. The Miniguns can carry out 'search' firing at 1,600 rounds per minute, increasing this to 4,000 rounds per minute in an attack. More than 1,000 HueyCobras have already been ordered for the US Army, and a twin-engined AH-1J SeaCobra version is being built for the US Marine Corps. The AH-1's small size and slim profile make it easy to conceal on the ground and difficult to hit in the air.

bombing offensive at North Vietnam which, in tonnage, surpassed their efforts against Germany in the second World War. They learned the frustration of trying to bomb a subsistence economy to a halt. They learned—at vast cost—the absurdity of risking a five-million-dollar Phantom against a five-hundred-dollar bamboo bridge. A Phantom lost was a Phantom lost, often with two valuable crewmen; a buckled bridge could be, and would be, rebuilt in a night, or at most in a week.

In their attempts to halt the southward flow of material into South Vietnam, along the winding Ho Chi Minh jungle trail, they sometimes had only trucks to hit. Often they were committing their multi-million-dollar F-4s and F-105s against 15-dollar bicycles. Cheap Chinese bikes, with special panniers to accommodate about 250 lb (113 kg) of stores were regularly pushed on their way south, unloaded and ridden north again along the trail. Small wonder that the Americans were reduced to desperate frustration, for how do you accomplish successful aerial interdiction against bicycles?

The bombing of North Vietnam eventually was stopped—the political odium, and the vast cost, were simply not offset by the lack of success at that period. US air effort returned to 'in-country' operations—within South Vietnam borders—and some-

times in neighbouring Cambodia and Laos. Air support for ground forces was the task.

Pre-eminently, this involved helicopters, operated (and lost) in their thousands and salvaged in their hundreds. Helicopters became the standard means of assault movement all over South Vietnam, and 'air cavalry' divisions were formed around their own organic helicopter fleets. With the assault helicopters, themselves carrying light sideways-firing guns to return often-deadly small-arms fire from the ground, went more-heavily-armed 'gunships' to prepare the way for airborne assaults. Initially the gunships were no more than the same types of helicopter mounting more armament, including grenade launchers and rocket pods, and from them evolved the attack helicopter, designed from the start as an actual weapon platform.

The first true gunship to enter service was the AH-1 HueyCobra, which itself used the dynamic components and power plant of the established UH-1 'Huey' series, married to a new, ultra-slim, two-seat fuselage of minimal frontal area. This, combined with higher speed, made it a more difficult target for the ground-based marksman to hit than the standard wide-body troop-carrying 'choppers'. The AH-1, and similar developments using existing power, transmission and rotor systems, were intended as interim measures until the true AAFSS

(advanced airborne fire suppression system) helicopter was available. This concept, represented for a time by the very fast, radical Lockheed Cheyenne, was plagued with development troubles and a new generation of advanced attack helicopters is not now expected in service before 1980.

The US air role in South Vietnam was essentially that of providing airlift and firepower for troops on the ground, and hitting constantly-shifting, small targets in dense jungle country, or in rice paddy and marshland. Other simple firing platforms had to be evolved to avoid committing sophisticated, supersonic jets to the fray. One was the 'Dragonship' or 'Spooky'—a ferociously-armed C-47 Dakota with three 6,000-rounds-a-minute Miniguns bristling through its port-side windows and aimed by the captain through a special left-seat sight. Similarly-armed AC-119 and AC-130 dragonship conversions followed, mounting heavier firepower for use against ground targets.

Other veteran types were in great demand as the intensity of the Vietnam war increased. The Douglas Skyraider, last operational piston-engined fighter-bomber with the USN, was valued highly for its ability to absorb tremendous anti-aircraft punishment (in marked contrast to modern jets) and still return safely home. The world was scoured for Skyraiders previously sold

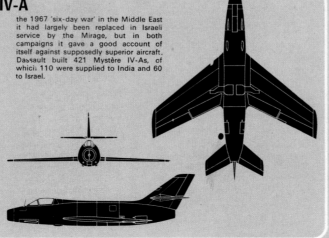

Above left: The adage 'simplify, and add lightness' is one which the US forces learned in Vietnam only at tremendous cost. In March 1968 six of the USAF's new swing-wing F-111A fighters arrived in Thailand; in the first week of operations two of them were lost, adding another unhappy chapter to the early story of this warplane, which did not prove its full worth until the last year of US involvement

Top: Major US attack aircraft was the 'Thud', or F-105D Thunderchief, although in general the use of such advanced and expensive aircraft was hardly justified by the results achieved

Above: Code-named 'Stinger', the Fairchild AC-119K was one of two gunship versions of this large transport aircraft operated in Vietnam. It has underwing jet pods to improve performance, and carries side-firing Miniguns and equipment for night operations

DASSAULT MYSTERE IV-A

Powered by: One 7,716 lb (3,500 kg) st Hispano-Suiza Verdon 350 turbojet engine
Wing span: 36 ft 5¾ in (11.12 m)
Length: 42 ft 1½ in (12.84 m)
Wing area: 344.4 sq ft (32.00 m²)
Gross weight: 18,700 lb (8,482 kg)
Max speed: 696 mph (1,120 km/h) at S/L
Range: 820 miles (1,320 km) with two underwing drop-tanks
Armament: Two 30-mm DEFA cannon (with 150 rpg) and pack of 55 unguided air-to-air rockets in fuselage; two 1,000-lb or four 500-lb bombs, two air-to-air or air-to-surface rocket packs or two napalm containers under the wings
Accommodation: Crew of 1
First flight: 28 September 1952
Developed from France's first production jet fighter, the straight-winged Ouragan, via the interim Mystère II-C, the Mystère IV-A entered service with the French Air Force in 1955. It first fired its guns in anger during the 1956 Suez crisis, both with French squadrons and with the Israeli Air Force, with which it was just beginning to enter service. By the time of

the 1967 'six-day war' in the Middle East it had largely been replaced in Israeli service by the Mirage, but in both campaigns it gave a good account of itself against supposedly superior aircraft. Dassault built 421 Mystère IV-As, of which 110 were supplied to India and 60 to Israel.

or given away to other nations as part of military aid, and they were much used as escort aircraft for rescue helicopters, the exploits of which form one of the more satisfying chapters in the American story in Vietnam.

The 'in-country' war proved to be one of ceaseless conflict against elusive, ever-moving guerilla forces, and needed to be one of constant surveillance, or quiet reconnaissance. Much radio monitoring and fixing of Vietcong transmissions was done by aircraft as small as O-1 Bird Dogs, skimming the matted jungle treetops with two enormous whip aerials on their wingtips. The same type, succeeded later, by the O-2 and the OV-10A, was the mainstay of ceaseless visual searching by the USAF's skilled forward air controllers—daily roaming the jungle, highly vulnerable to small-arms fire from below—watching for signs of enemy encampments, movements and stores. When they found them, they stayed close in over the target while calling in and directing air strikes against them; and they continued to linger—to make an assessment of the damage wrought.

The early in-country combination of tiny piston-engined O-1 and supersonic F-100 Super Sabre fighter-bomber gave way first to lighter jet aircraft such as the F-5 and the A-37, and later to a new class of aircraft doing both jobs. With total air superiority the speed, the high ceiling, the complexity and cost of the modern jet fighter are not required for such action against guerilla forces, however able. So again, the attack helicopter has prospered, together with such combined FAC/attack aircraft as the twin-turboprop OV-10A. Now, after several years of project studies, there are other relatively-low-cost attack aircraft and 'bomb trucks' on the stocks to meet the USAF's AX air support requirement.

In the catch-as-catch-can war in Vietnam, there was much emphasis on quiet aircraft for the electronic monitoring, for 24 hours a day, of forces infiltrating over borders and along jungle paths. The quiet-aircraft programmes started from a quiet and logical point—gliders—and resulted in trials with powered adaptations of production gliders, packed with electronics, including such sensors as 'people sniffers' which can detect the presence of human beings by sensing the exuding of sweat from quite incredible heights and distances. Climbing high and gliding for long periods with power off, or cruising under power from muffled engines fitted with 'whispering' low-speed paddle-bladed propellers, these almost silent listeners had some success in Vietnam and further developments, including unmanned drone versions, are in hand.

Conventional medium- and high-level heavy bombing operations involved originally the despatch of big formations of the USAF's B-52 strategic bombers over the 5,000 mile (8,050 km) route from Okinawa and Guam and carpet-bombing areas of jungle designated as Vietcong war zones. The measured success was minimal in proportion to the immense cost involved.

Another costly lesson was learned from 'Operation Ranch-hand'—the systematic defoliation of jungle to deprive the enemy of cover and, incidentally, the destruction of crops when they were likely to sustain the enemy. Fairchild C-123 Providers, fitted with big tanks and spray bars, were the instrument for this—and few would have envied the job of the aircrew flying these bulky transports on low, slow, pre-determined paths, in neat echelon formations, immediately over jungle covering hostile forces. Happy was the enemy gunner presented with such a target—four or five big, slow aircraft in a steady, undeviating cruise not far overhead. Even if he missed one, he was almost certain to get the one behind.

If there are lessons to be learned from the Vietnam war it is that absolute military might is no answer to determined indigenous guerillas enjoying a substantial measure of local support, when the strategic balance of the world—the balance of terror—is such that the fear of nuclear retribution prevents the exercise of that might. Heavy bombers, supersonic fighters and even clattering gunships have only a limited effect against highly-mobile, ever-moving jungle forces. And such disasters as Operation Ranch-hand, such political hot potatoes as defoliation, 'destroy and burn', free-fire zones and widespread napalm attacks, lose more international and local support than their military objectives justify.

Aviation technology can help to gain 'intelligence' in this kind of war; it is essential for mobility; and, at quite modest levels, exemplified by the gunship, it can bring into play the firepower that may, on occasions, be needed. But it can be no substitute—as, tragically, the Americans for too long thought it could—for determined, well-trained forces sweating, stalking, hitting and pacifying on the ground.

All that a further round of heavy bombing could achieve in the end—with targets in the North instead of in the jungles—was a cease-fire which permitted the withdrawal of US forces.

As far as the technology is concerned, Vietnam brings one back to the old adage: 'simplify, and add lightness'. One feels that it is a lesson the Israelis would have understood, instinctively, all the time.

Above: The Douglas Skyraider was on the verge of being retired from service when the Korean War broke out in 1950. Instead, it stayed to become one of the greatest work-horses not only of that conflict but of the even more demanding war in Vietnam. This picture shows an A-1E of the USAF armed with eight 250-lb (113-kg) general-purpose bombs and four 20-mm guns

Left: American troops in Vietnam signal 'all clear' for incoming helicopters to land in a jungle clearing. These four are Bell UH-1 Iroquois, one of the most widely-used of all 'choppers' in that theatre of operations

Below left: One of the USAF's largest helicopters is the Sikorsky HH-3E. Built for the Aerospace Rescue and Recovery Service, it has armour plating, jettisonable fuel tanks, a rescue hoist and a gigantic refuelling probe

Overleaf: The 1,400 mph (2,250 km/h) Phantom is one of the most versatile military aeroplanes in service today. Its main roles are those of air defence fighter, low-level strike, and tactical reconnaissance. Phantoms equipping British squadrons have Rolls-Royce Spey turbofan engines, but otherwise differ only in detail from their counterparts in US service

TACTICAL AIR POWER

Skimming the tree-tops, so low that the airfield radar has failed entirely to detect their approach, six Phantom FGR.2 ground-attack fighters of the RAF's No 6 Squadron slam their way across the airfield. Even the roar of their twin Rolls-Royce Spey engines is drowned by the bursting bombs, rockets and napalm incendiary weapons that mark with yellow and red flame, and great billowing clouds of black smoke, the path that the aircraft followed over the runways and lines of combat aircraft that were parked near them.

The destruction is so complete that the air base is of no further use to its original occupants. To encourage their evacuation to a safer spot, eight Wessex HC.2 helicopters of No 72 Squadron drop down between the fires and craters to disgorge members of No 2 Squadron of the RAF Regiment. Having dealt with the last glimmers of enemy resistance, these men

disappear, surprisingly, into a nearby wood. The mystery is soon solved as four Harrier GR.1s of No 1 Squadron settle neatly into small clearings between the trees, their vertical take-off and landing (VTOL) capability making them independent of the shattered runways. There, the RAF Regiment personnel prepare to service them for further action—and to defend them if necessary, for this spot is well inside former enemy territory.

Meanwhile an Andover twin-turboprop transport of 46 Squadron has succeeded in landing on the grass between the holes left by stray bombs, its reverse-pitch propellers bringing it to a stop after an astonishingly short run. Almost before it is stationary, drums of fuel are being rolled down its rear loading ramp and put into cargo nets which are then hauled to the waiting Harriers by the Wessex helicopters. Huge quantities of other supplies and

ammunition are brought in by four Hercules C.1 heavy transports of 47 Squadron. Instead of landing, they pass over the crippled airfield at a height of between 5 and 20 ft (1.5-6 m.) and a steady speed of 145-155 mph (233-250 km/h), while parachutes drag their loads out of the open freight-holds on crash-proof platforms that smack to the ground behind them. Seldom has any air-drop delivered its goods more precisely to where they are needed.

Before long, the Harriers, refuelled and re-armed, climb out of their hides in the wood, form up over the airfield in sections of two, and race away at a shade below the speed of sound to eliminate targets to which they have been directed by ground controllers.

It is all very slick—a perfect example of how an air force can take advantage of all the most advanced ideas in combat aircraft design, integrated strike/transport units

Above: Another view of the Mirage G with its swing-wing in the fully-swept, high-speed cruising position

Below, left: First fixed-wing V/STOL aircraft to enter service anywhere in the world, the Hawker Siddeley Harrier is shown here in the insignia of the US Marine Corps, which operates the type for the all-important close support role

Above right: When there are difficult tasks to be done in almost inaccessible places, the helicopter is unrivalled. This Royal Navy Wessex is delivering coils of barbed wire to a defence post atop a hill in jungle territory in Borneo, during the confrontation with Indonesia in the early 'sixties

Right: Despite their comparatively low speed, helicopters offer no easy target for ground fire. By flying low, they can take advantage of every scrap of natural cover. Most carry guns or rockets for defence and to 'keep down the heads' of the opposition while they put down their loads in front-line areas

Far right: One of the most controversial combat aircraft ever flown, the F-111—here seen with its swing-wing in an intermediate position —was expected to fulfil an impossible number of different roles. The first Wing of F-111E tactical fighters to be deployed overseas began to form at Upper Heyford, England, in September 1970

and delivery techniques, to snatch a forward base and put it to use. The operation described took place before tens of thousands of spectators at the 1970 SBAC Display at Farnborough—without, of course, actual bombs, rockets and napalm ploughing up the airfield, but none the less convincing.

At the time the RAF was the only air force in the world capable of giving such a demonstration of modern tactical air power in action, because it was the only one with a VTOL combat aircraft in the class of the Harrier. To be strictly correct, this pioneer 'jump-jet' should be referred to as a V/STOL type, the 'S' signifying that it can utilise a very short take-off run, as opposed to helicopter-like vertical ascent, when there is room to do so. This permits a big increase in the load of weapons or fuel that

it can carry, and is important, as this ability to take off vertically demands so much power that the Harrier could carry only a fairly modest weapon load in its initial form.

Already engine power is being increased rapidly and each rise adds to the attractiveness of the aircraft, which is being built for the US Marine Corps and Spanish Navy as well as the RAF. One day, it may be in as much demand as its predecessor, the Hunter, which has such outstanding performance as a close support fighter-bomber, to back up troops on the ground, and as a trainer for such work, that new fuselages had to be built, many years after the original production line closed down.

This emphasises the fact that the highest possible performance, in terms of speeds, is not always the most important factor in assessing the worth of a tactical combat aeroplane. Much depends on the task to be

undertaken, for this category of military aviation covers an immense variety of jobs.

In brief, tactical air power is concerned with the support of short-term operations in and around a combat area. The United States Air Force Dictionary defines it as: 'air combat action carried out in support of, or co-operation with, surface forces engaging the enemy. Applied to air-to-air combat and air strikes aimed at achieving air superiority, to air interdiction, to battle-area reconnaissance, and to bombing and strafing attacks upon battle area ground targets.' Thus the Battle of Britain was a tactical operation, as the *Luftwaffe* had the short-term objective of softening up the defences and eliminating air opposition in advance of the projected invasion of England by German ground forces. When it was defeated, the subsequent night offensive against London and other cities was a *strategic* operation, with the inten-

tion of wearing down the capability and will of the British people as a whole to continue the war. The later British and American 'round-the-clock' bomber offensive against Germany was a further clear example of a strategic operation, lasting several years.

Most kinds of tactical air combat were pioneered in World War I. From the first days of that war, reconnaissance aircraft observed, and later photographed in vast detail, the movements of enemy armies on the ground. They watched and corrected the fire of their own artillery in front-line areas. So important were the consequences of such support for the land battle that fighter aircraft were evolved primarily to shoot down or drive away the reconnaissance machines. Tactical bombers then entered the picture to attack the airfields from which enemy aircraft operated, as well as army headquarters, front-line

positions and road, rail and other communications targets in the immediate battle area. The term 'interdiction' was coined to describe this last function of tactical air power, meaning 'the action of making it very difficult for the enemy to move from one place to another.

From such commitments emerged the fighter-bomber and dive-bomber. Fighter-to-fighter 'dogfights', although they occurred on a large scale, were not an end in themselves. They resulted from the need to prevent enemy fighters from interfering with one's own reconnaissance, artillery spotting and bombing activities.

Tactical operations were by no means confined to the land battle, even in 1914-18. Over the waters around the coastline of the United Kingdom, the landplanes, seaplanes and flying-boats of the RNAS hunted and attacked the German Zeppelin airships that shadowed and bombed Allied

naval forces, and evolved complex search 'patterns' that made it difficult for surfaced submarines to pass undetected and unopposed through the narrow seas. Such operations, and the harassing of enemy shipping, were all part of the tactical air picture.

In the early 'twenties, the RAF was made responsible for keeping the peace in Iraq—a part of the world where dissident tribesmen regarded raiding, murder and general trouble-making as a logical and rather enjoyable ingredient of everyday life. With eight squadrons of aircraft, mostly of World War I vintage, and a mixed brigade of British and Indian infantry, some native levies, and four squadrons of armoured cars manned by the RAF, the air force replaced some 33 battalions of infantry, six of cavalry and 16 batteries of artillery.

The experiment, like similar 'air control' operations elsewhere in the world, was a

tremendous success. The mere threat of air attack, contained in warning messages dropped over troublesome villages, was often sufficient to maintain relative peace. If the attack became necessary, advance warning normally enabled the tribesmen to take to the country before the bombers arrived, so that they suffered the temporary inconvenience of loss of home comfort and means of livelihood rather than their lives. It was far more humane, and led to far less bloodshed, than the old method of dealing with the troublemakers by sending army units to fight them.

It also emphasised for the first time the vital fact that transport aircraft could play in tactical operations, by putting down small parties of highly-trained troops where they were needed, quickly and without the fatigue of a forced march through difficult and hostile country before any action that had to be fought.

Unfortunately, the fact that such campaigns were usually waged against an enemy equipped with primitive weapons, and entirely lacking in air defences, played

into the hands of penny-pinching politicians. There was an increasing concentration on general-purpose aircraft—bombers that could also be used for reconnaissance and for picking up messages from the ground with hooks mounted under their fuselage; and transports that could carry and drop a few light bombs, instead of proper heavy bombers. Such machines were quite useless when opposed by or compared with uncompromised genuine fighters and bombers, and this is still true in the modern, supersonic jet age.

For an example there is no need to look further than one of the most expensive and potentially-promising tactical combat aircraft ever devised, the American 'swing-wing' General Dynamics F-111. To cut costs, the US Defense Department decided that different versions of this one basic design could be adapted to serve as a tactical fighter-bomber, a reconnaissance aircraft and a strategic bomber with the US Air Force, and as a fleet defence interceptor with the US Navy. Entering into the spirit of things, and impressed by the

enthusiasm of the F-111's protagonists, both the RAF and Royal Australian Air Force decided that this 1,450 mph (2,330 km/h) design, with its planned weapon load of up to 31,000 lb (14,060 kg), would meet their urgent needs for new strike aircraft to replace ageing bomber forces. By the mid-sixties, the makers of the F-111 were looking forward confidently to selling at least 1,608 of the aircraft at a cost of anything from £6 million to £8.6 million each, including spares and technical support.

Alas, the F-111 was not to fulfil its multi-role promise. The US Navy and RAF cancelled their versions; the Australians were persuaded to take Phantom fighter-bombers for a while, until the aircraft had got over its troubles. Entry into service was delayed by structural failures and other problems, and orders were cut progressively and drastically on account of both the technical problems and rising costs.

Other projects for tactical combat aircraft have fared no better. Britain's TSR.2 and

Left: RAF Strike Command's first squadron of Nimrod maritime patrol aircraft with, in foreground, one of the piston-engined Shackletons which these superb combat machines

Above and right: The US Navy counterpart to the Nimrod, the Lockheed P-3 Orion, developed from the Electra airliner. The tail 'sting' on such aircraft encloses Magnetic Anomaly Detection gear to locate submerged submarines. Submarine attack weapons carried by the US Navy's Orion include rockets fired from wingtip launchers. Its fuselage weapon bay and underwing attachments can also accommodate a heavy load of depth bombs, mines, torpedoes and missiles

Left: Italy's single-seat Agusta A 106 light helicopter, powered by a 330 hp turboshaft engine, is one of the smallest manned submarine chasers yet flown. In addition to search devices, it can carry one or two homing torpedoes under its fuselage

Right : First of the new AWACS (airborne warning and control system) aircraft, designed to locate incoming attack aircraft and direct interceptors towards them, is Russia's converted Tu-114 transport, known to NATO as 'Moss'. Its search radar is carried inside a huge 'saucer' fairing above the cabin

Right lower: Russia is one of the few nations which still finds a first-line job for flying-boats. This turboprop-powered Beriev M-12 (Be-12) amphibian equips an anti-submarine squadron of the Red Banner Northern Fleet. It has a nose-mounted search radar and underwing weapon attachments

Far right: Grumman's highly successful OV-1B Mohawk turboprop-powered observation aircraft carries side-looking radar in a long under-fuselage container. This provides a permanent radar photographic map of terrain on either side of the flight path

the Anglo - French variable - geometry (swing-wing) programmes were both axed for economic reasons. In their place, the RAF, like the *Luftwaffe,* is now pinning its hopes on the international Panavia MRCA—the latest attempt to produce a general - purpose Multi - Role Combat Aircraft. Original plans to produce both single- and two-seat versions, for every possible job from short-range air defence to long-range strike, did not progress far. The single-seater was soon abandoned and total orders for the British, German and Italian air forces were cut from 1,185 to a possible 810 aircraft, of which the first flew in the summer of 1974. Cancellation of the single-seater persuaded the Germans that they should work with France to evolve a dual-purpose trainer/light attack aircraft to fill the gap.

So, the immense variety of tactical combat types continues and is unlikely to become smaller in the years ahead. There have to be highly-supersonic tactical strike and reconnaissance aircraft, fighter-bombers and a vast range of transport aircraft

for first-line duties in major war zones. In places where enemy air defence is limited, it is possible to use helicopter 'gunships', transports converted to take batteries of multi-barrel guns for heavy and concentrated ground - attack, and compara - tively slow, manoeuvrable close support types like the Rockwell OV-10 Bronco. Increasingly, these tactical types will make use of VTOL, V/STOL or STOL techniques to make them independent of fixed, easily-destroyed bases.

Over the sea, the growing menace of the missile-carrying nuclear submarine, in particular, demands the availability of complex aircraft like the Nimrod, packed with electronics to hunt their prey and armed with elaborate missiles and weapons to destroy any submarine that is located. Such aircraft must be backed up with high-speed strike aircraft capable of sinking both surface ships and submarines, and by ship-borne anti-submarine helicopters, supplemented or replaced eventually by VTOL aircraft like the Harrier.

A dozen industries collaborate with the

aircraft industry in producing such machines, with a particularly heavy burden falling on the electronics industry. A modern strike aircraft must be able to find its way to any prescribed target under virtually automatic, self-contained control, leaving its crew free to concentrate on tactics. It must be able to locate and destroy the target at night or in bad weather, and counter or jam the enemy defensive radar that is trying to locate it and guide fighters and missiles to destroy it. Equally, the defences must try to beat its electronic countermeasures and put their own fighters in a position to attack the intruder, perhaps with the help of big AWACS (airborne warning and control system) aircraft, circling ceaselessly at 20,000 ft (6,100 m) or higher and processing data received continuously from a huge radar in a 'saucer' fairing above the fuselage.

Tactical combat flying has come a long way since the French sent up the first frail balloons, at the end of a cable, to observe the movement of enemy armies in the 18th century.

Top: OV-10A Bronco was designed specifically for light armed reconnaissance and counter-insurgency duties in places like Vietnam. Its manoeuvrability and modest speed well suit it for finding and marking targets for attack by jets in forward areas

Above left: Ground attack demands manoeuvrability and precision rather than sheer speed. For that reason, Cavalier Aircraft put back into production versions of the Mustang fighter of World War II, using a mixture of war-surplus and new components. Operators include nations receiving military aid from the USA. Russia's small, fast helicopter carrier, the *Moskva*, is pioneering a new concept for anti-submarine warfare and, possibly, the close support of landing parties. It is equipped initially with Kamov Ka-25 helicopters, of which four are seen here hovering above its deck. With V/STOL aircraft like Britain's Harrier, its potency would be increased enormously

Above right: Nigeria is one of many young nations in Africa which have received combat aircraft of Russian design. Il-28 twin-jet bombers and MiG-17 fighters, like the two shown here, were supplied by Egypt during the war with the breakaway state of Biafra

Below: Evolved from the F-8 Crusader naval fighter, the Vought A-7E Corsair II is a tremendously effective light attack aircraft powered by an Allison TF41 turbofan (American-built Rolls-Royce Spey). It has a near-sonic speed and can carry several tons of external weapons

STRATEGIC MILITARY AIR POWER

Top: Few aircraft have caused greater surprise than Russia's Tu-20 bomber, known to NATO as 'Bear'. Until it was first seen in 1955, the fastest turboprop aeroplanes were thought to be limited to about 425 mph (684 km/h); yet the Tu-20 has an over-target speed of 500 mph (805 km/h) at 41,000 ft (12,500 m) and range of 7,800 miles (12,550 km) with an eleven-ton bomb load. It is shown here in its latest maritime reconnaissance version

Right: No picture could symbolise better the deterrent policy made possible by strategic air power. For many post-war years the world was kept free of major war by the sheltering wings of bombers like the Vulcan, armed with air-to-surface nuclear missiles

Strategic air power, in the shape of two B-29 Superfortresses carrying rather primitive atomic bombs, brought a sudden end to World War II in August 1945. In doing so they removed all need for an Allied invasion of the Japanese home islands, which might well have cost millions of casualties among the armed forces of both sides and the civilian population of Japan.

What befell the people of Hiroshima and Nagasaki, upon whom those two bombs fell more than a quarter of a century ago, was horrible and heart-breaking. Even today, it is impossible to look at photographs of a shadow on a wall—a kind of photographic image that was the only remaining trace of an atomised human being—without feelings of revulsion. Yet it is because of what happened to those Japanese cities that the world has been free of major war for so long. Only the

deterrent policy of 'peace through fear' prevented the Berlin Air Lift of 1948/49, the Korean War of 1950/53 and the Cuban missile crisis of 1962 from escalating into an armed clash between east and west. In fact, the power of nuclear weapons has increased to such a degree since 1945 that the whole concept of major war has

become unthinkable, as it would initiate the obliteration of entire communities and countries on both sides.

If this sounds an extravagant claim, one need only remember that Britain's first H-bomb, back in the 'fifties, was equivalent to one million tons of TNT and that all the destruction rained on Europe by the

RAF and USAAF in World War II was caused by just two million tons of bombs.

In little more than half a century, therefore, the aeroplane has exerted a most profound influence on the lives of everyone in the world, by offering the choice of annihilation on a scale that makes the plagues of the Middle Ages seem mild by comparison, or all the opportunities for a better, fuller life that derive from large-scale air travel and the vast increase in foodstuffs for a hungry world made possible by aerial seeding, top-dressing (fertiliser-spreading) and crop-spraying with pest-killers.

The dictionary defines strategic air operations as those 'aimed at the enemy's military, industrial, political and economic system, or at massive undermining of morale'. The operations include, we are told, 'strategic reconnaissance, strategic air transport, strategic fighter operations, and the employment of strategic missiles, as well as strategic bombing.'

There is nothing new in this concept. One of the earliest true stories in the recorded history of aviation tells of the strange 'flying boat' devised by Father Francesco de Lana-Terzi in the year 1670. When it proved impracticable, he commented that perhaps this was not surprising, since 'God would surely never allow such a machine to be successful, since . . . no city would be proof against surprise, as the ship could at any time be brought above its squares, or even the courtyards of its dwellings, and come to earth so that its crew could land. In the case of ships that sail the sea, the aerial ship could be made to descend from the upper air to the level of their sails so

the rigging could be cut. Or even without descending so low, iron weights could be hurled down to wreck the ships and kill their crews; or the ships could be set on fire by fireballs and bombs. Not only ships, but houses, fortresses and cities could thus be destroyed, with the certainty that the air-ship would come to no harm, as the missiles could be thrown from a great height.'

Few of the world's military leaders were to share de Lana's far-sighted views on the potential of tactical and strategic air power for nearly $2\frac{1}{2}$ centuries after he recorded them. The first World War changed all that.

An element of good fortune must have helped Flt Lt R L G Marix of the RNAS to destroy a large airship shed at Dusseldorf, complete with Zeppelin Z.9 inside, when he dropped on it a few tiny 20-lb (9-kg) bombs from a Sopwith Tabloid on 8 October 1914. But there was nothing haphazard about the later strategic bomber offensives by the British, French, German, Italian and Russian air forces in that war. By 1918 the newly-formed Royal Air Force had bombs weighing up to 1,650 lb (748 kg) each; and the Independent Force had achieved such excellent results with its four squadrons of Handley Page O/100 and O/400 night bombers, single squadron of F.E.2bs and four squadrons of de Havilland day bombers that its leader, the future Marshal of the Royal Air Force Lord Trenchard, determined that the whole post-war policy of the RAF would be built on the foundation of strategic bombing.

There were times when the foundations

This page, top: Many B-52 Stratofortress bombers of the USAF Strategic Air Command (SAC) exchanged their standard grey and white colour scheme for a coat of camouflage when deployed to take part in operations in Vietnam

Above: After being retired from service as strategic bombers, Handley Page Victors continued to perform two vitally important duties with the Royal Air Force. This Victor B(SR)Mk 2 was used by No 543 strategic reconnaissance squadron, based at RAF Wyton. Other Victors have been converted into flight refuelling tankers, able to service up to three aircraft at a time

Opposite page, top: Each Boeing EC-135C 'Looking Glass' flying command post contains a miniaturised version of the SAC control centre at Offutt Air Force Base. If ground control were put out of action, the EC-135s could direct SAC's entire force of strategic bombers and ICBMs

Bottom: Lockheed's U-2—one of the most remarkable and best-known strategic reconnaissance aircraft yet sent into action. Two years after its flights over Russia were stopped, it discovered Soviet missiles in Cuba

BOEING B-52 STRATOFORTRESS

Powered by: Eight 17,000 lb (7,711 kg) st Pratt & Whitney TF33-P-3 turbofan engines
Wing span: 185 ft 0 in (56.42 m)
Length: 156 ft 0 in (47.55 m)
Wing area: 4,000 sq ft (371.6 m²)
Gross weight: 488,000 lb (221,350 kg)
Max speed: approx 660 mph (1,062 km/h) at 20,000 ft (6,100 m)
Max range: 12,500 miles (20,120 km)
Armament: One 20-mm remote-controlled multi-barrel cannon in tail; bombs and Quail diversionary missiles internally; two Hound Dog air-to-surface missiles and ALE-25 diversionary rocket pods under wings
Accommodation: Crew of 6
First flight (YB-52): 15 April 1952
The first operational version of the B-52 entered service in mid-1955, although development of the design had begun ten years earlier, shortly after the end of the war in Europe. It has been continually refined and developed, the major version numerically being the B-52G with greater fuel tankage and range and able to carry Hound Dog 'stand-off' nuclear weapons. The data apply to the B-52H, the final production version.

This B-52 Stratofortress carries under its inner wings a pair of AGM-28 Hound Dog air-to-surface missiles, each armed with an H-bomb warhead. In its bomb-bay are free-fall nuclear weapons and ADM-20 Quail diversionary missiles, each of which gives the same radar 'echo' as the bomber when released as a decoy to counter enemy defences

Below, opposite page: Tu-16 (NATO 'Badger') maritime reconnaissance bombers, like these machines of the Soviet Northern Fleet, utilise a unique wingtip-to-wingtip flight refuelling technique to increase their range. The attachments under the wings of the receiver aircraft (top in photo) normally carry electronic pods

Centre, top: Original plans to buy 210 swing-wing FB-111A strategic bombers, to replace the supersonic B-58 Hustlers and early versions of the Stratofortress in service with SAC, were cut as a result of troubles experienced with the F-111. Nonetheless, the 76 FB-111As delivered to the USAF are formidable aircraft, each able to carry up to fifty 750-lb (340-kg) bombs

Centre bottom: The twin-jet Tupolev Tu-22 (NATO 'Blinder') was Russia's first supersonic strategic bomber, with an estimated speed of Mach 1.4. Like the earlier Tu-16 and Tu-20, it is used extensively for maritime reconnaissance

Below: The NKC-135A is one of many conversions of the Boeing KC-135 Stratotanker design used for unspecified special reconnaissance and other duties with the USAF. Such aircraft carry radar and other sensors in pods and blisters, with batteries of cameras and other equipment inside their cabins

began to look a trifle insecure. In the early 'twenties, the Vimys of D Flight, No 100 Squadron at Spittlegate were the only multi-engined bombers in service in the UK. However, there were others overseas, where even the wartime O/400 could still impress. In *The Seven Pillars of Wisdom*, T E Lawrence tells how: 'At Um el Surab the Handley stood majestic on the grass, with Bristols and 9a, like fledglings beneath its spread of wings. Round it admired the Arabs, saying: "Indeed, and at last, they have sent us THE aeroplane, of which these things were foals." '.

Between wars, the Germans and Russians, in particular, did not share the belief of Trenchard in the absolute importance of strategic bombing. Unlike the RAF, which was the first major air service to be completely independent of the army and navy, their air arms were intended primarily for the tactical close support of the army. It was because of this basic policy that the Soviet air force did so little strategic bombing in World War II, while the *Luftwaffe* was so obsessed with tactical operations that even the big four-engined Heinkel He 177 bomber, which entered service in 1943, had to be structurally strong enough for dive-bombing. It proved to be one of the enemy aircraft

industry's greatest failures of the war, while the Allied bomber forces relentlessly pounded the German homeland, and Japan, towards defeat.

Up to 1945, the might of a bomber force was measured in terms of the number of aircraft it operated, and their quality. Following perfection of the first atomic bombs, numbers became less significant. A single large bomber, armed with three such weapons, could eliminate three cities in a single sortie, with the destructive power of the bombs growing all the time as A-bombs gave way to H-bombs and then bigger H-bombs. It became a matter of simply ensuring that the single bomber *would* reach its target, in the face of steadily-more-sophisticated defence systems.

The greatest period of the bomber's career was probably in the mid-sixties, when the RAF's V-force was at its peak. No strategic attack aircraft in the world was more formidable than the Vulcan B.2. Cruising just below the speed of sound at well over 50,000 ft (15,250 m), it was a target beyond the capability of most fighters to intercept, particularly when its electronic countermeasures (ECM) devices were operating. Some of these are still secret. Suffice it to say that they were capable of nullifying enemy radar and radio transmissions over a large area

around and beneath the aircraft, so that it could not be found by ground radar or airborne radar on night fighters. If an enemy interceptor or ground forces succeeded in launching an infra-red homing missile in the Vulcan's direction, a decoy device lured the weapon off course to detonate harmlessly far from the bomber.

So mighty, and inviolable, was the V-force of Vulcans and Victors, armed with Blue Steel H-bomb missiles and free-fall atomic weapons, that Bomber Command had no hesitation in claiming that it could destroy 80 per cent of the worth-while strategic targets in the Soviet Union by itself.

Even bearing in mind the great advances made in missile defence systems in the past five years, it is probable that sufficient strategic bombers could be flown to any target to ensure its destruction, by flying low (beneath most ground radar cover) and by using the latest ECM and long-range air-launched missiles. However, the German V-2 rocket of 1944-45 pointed to a much simpler and easier way of doing the job. That is why manned bomber forces have been supplemented, in some cases replaced completely, by thermonuclear (H-bomb) missiles, stored in underground 'silo' launchers and on difficult-to-find submarines.

The complexity of some of these missiles by comparison with the V-2 is equivalent to comparing the Concorde with the Wright biplane of 1903. They can travel anything from 6,000 to 10,000 miles (9,650-16,000 km) with a warhead that re-enters the Earth's atmosphere at 22 times the speed of sound. To reduce the effectiveness of the anti-missile missiles (ABMs) that neither the USA nor the Soviet Union can afford to deploy in worthwhile numbers, the warheads carry decoys to lure away the ABMs. Some are manoeuvrable in the atmosphere and divide into three separate H-bomb charges to attack three targets simultaneously. One type, launched by the Soviet SS-9 missile, is known as the fractional orbital bombardment system (FOBS) because it can travel round the world like a satellite in a 100-mile (160 km) high orbit until it approaches the target, whereupon it can be directed out of orbit for its attack. One type of multiple independently-targeted re-entry vehicle (MIRV) developed by the Russians for the FOBS, and for the standard SS-9 intercontinental ballistic missile (ICBM), has three separate warheads intended to fall in such a pattern that they match precisely the distances apart of each American Minuteman ICBM 'silo' in a three-missile cluster.

How do we know this? Remember that strategic air power includes not only attack but reconnaissance. World War II, in particular, proved that a bomber offensive attained its full effectiveness only when the planners could despatch photo-reconnaissance aircraft to bring back up-to-the-minute pictures of the target and its defences. Equally important was post-attack coverage, to evaluate the degree of destruction and determine whether or not further attacks were needed.

Modern strategic reconnaissance makes the spy world of James Bond seem tame by comparison. The sort of piloted overflight that ended so disastrously over Russia for Gary Powers and his U-2 spyplane, in 1960, is now performed mainly by satellites; but flights around the perimeters of other countries, outside territorial limits, still go on day and night, in east and west, probing military secrets such as the types of radio and radar in use by the defences and taking conventional, infra-red and radar photographs far beyond the 'other side's' borders.

Information obtained in such ways told the western nations, and the Soviet Union, of the imminence of each of China's nuclear weapon tests and the launch of its first 'song-singing' satellite. So these caused no surprises in military circles. Similarly, the data provided by satellites, coupled with official warnings by the Soviet authorities that shipping should stay away from a certain area in the Pacific for a few days, always sets in motion a major US reconnaissance operation. Specially-converted C-135 aircraft, basically similar to a Boeing 707 airliner but festooned with electronic blisters and aerials and packed with cameras, take off at intervals for long patrols near the designated area of the Pacific where Soviet missile warheads will re-enter the atmosphere and drop into the sea. When a warhead is located, cameras lock on to it—and

that is how we know so much about the Russian MIRVs!

Attack . . . reconnaissance . . . and strategic transport—the third major arm of strategic air power. As in the 'twenties, there are many situations which do not call for destruction of the opposition. It may be that the political situation gets a little out of hand, as it did in Anguilla in 1969. A force of transport aircraft, carrying troops, police and equipment, can not only help to restore the situation but can initiate the building of roads and other facilities to improve the lot of the local people and reduce the grounds for further trouble.

In peace or war, a nation with overseas commitments needs to move men and stores rapidly and constantly over great distances. This need has produced the world's biggest transport aircraft, like the American C-5A Galaxy and the Soviet An-22 Antheus. When Peru suffered its disastrous earthquake in 1970, the An-22s joined other aircraft of many nations in flying vast quantities of relief to the victims. This, too, was modern strategic air power in action—power not only to wage war but primarily to prevent war and make life better for everyone, everywhere.

Right: Largest transport aircraft in Soviet service is the Antonov An-22 (NATO 'Cock'). Powered by four 15,000 shp NK-12MA turboprops, it will haul a payload of nearly 80 tons and is so big that entry is via doors in the wheel fairings

Below: Ten Short Belfast C Mk 1s were built for strategic transport duties with the RAF and have been in service since 1966. Each carries up to 78,000 lb (35,400 kg) of freight, including the largest types of guns, vehicles and missiles used by the British Army and RAF

Opposite page, centre: The USAF's largest turboprop transport is the Douglas C-133B Cargomaster, powered by four 7,500 shp T34 engines. Fifty Cargomasters were built, each able to carry a crew of ten and 200 troops or about 50 tons of freight

Opposite page, bottom: The USAF's Lockheed C-5A Galaxy transport is the largest aeroplane yet flown anywhere in the world. Eighty-one are on order, each able to carry nearly 120 tons of freight and with a maximum speed of 571 mph (919 km/h)

Below: Like most modern military transports, the Belfast has a hinged ramp-door at the rear of its cabin for speedy loading and for the air-dropping of freight. This photograph shows a Saladin armoured car driving out

INDEX
OF NAMES AND ILLUSTRATIONS

References in bold figures, thus: **66**, *indicate an illustration. References in italic, thus:* *45*, *indicate that the subject is described in a 'data box', with a silhouette. Aircraft featured in 'data boxes' are also listed separately at the end of the Index.*